Lecture Notes in Business Information Processing 54

Series Editors

Martin Nordio   Mathai Joseph
Bertrand Meyer   Andrey Terekhov (Eds.)

Software Engineering Approaches for Offshore and Outsourced Development

4th International Conference, SEAFOOD 2010
St. Petersburg, Russia, June 17-18, 2010
Proceedings

Springer

Volume Editors

Martin Nordio
ETH Zurich
8092 Zurich, Switzerland
E-mail: martin.nordio@inf.ethz.ch

Mathai Joseph
Tata Consulting Services
Pune 411 001, India
E-mail: m.joseph@tcs.com

Bertrand Meyer
ETH Zurich and Eiffel Software
8092 Zurich, Switzerland
E-mail: Bertrand.Meyer@inf.ethz.ch

Andrey Terekhov
Saint Petersburg State University and Lanit-Tercom
199034 St. Petersburg, Russia
E-mail: andrey.terekhov@lanit-tercom.com

Library of Congress Control Number: 2010928834

ACM Computing Classification (1998): K.6, D.2

ISSN	1865-1348
ISBN-10	3-642-13783-0 Springer Berlin Heidelberg New York
ISBN-13	978-3-642-13783-9 Springer Berlin Heidelberg New York

springer.com

Printed in Germany

Typesetting: Camera-ready by author, data conversion by Scientific Publishing Services, Chennai, India
Printed on acid-free paper 06/3180 5 4 3 2 1 0

Preface

Today's software production is increasingly distributed. Gone are the days of one-company, one-site projects; most industrial developments involve teams split over locations, countries, and cultures. This distribution poses new challenges, for example, how to develop the software requirements specification, and how to manage the project. These challenges are formidable; many failures have been reported in outsourced and distributed projects, often due not to lack of technical expertise, but to difficulties in management and communication.

SEAFOOD 2010, the fourth international conference on Software Engineering Advances For Outsourced and Offshore Development, was held in Peterhof (Saint Petersburg), Russia, on 17-18 June 2010. SEAFOOD 2010 provided an opportunity for participants from academia and industry to confront experiences, ideas and proposals. The submissions received covered a wide range of topics, from country-wide reports from Russia and Argentina to global project management. This volume includes 8 papers (4 full papers and 4 short papers) from the conference, selected after review by the Program Committee. The program also included two keynote presentations and the extended abstracts are included in this volume: "A Smarter Way: The Software Engineering Method and Theory Initiative (Semat)", by Ivar Jacobson, and "The Consortium for IT Software Quality", by Richard Mark Soley and Bill Curtis.

Many people contributed to SEAFOOD 2010. We thank the Program Committee and the external reviewers for their excellent work in reviewing and selecting the papers. The role of Andrei Voronkov's EasyChair conference system is gratefully acknowledged.

Iakov Kirilenko from Saint Petersburg State University and Lanit-Tercom and Nadia Polikarpova from ETH Zurich played a key role in organizing the conference; we are also grateful to Claudia Günthart for her organizational support.

May 2010

Martin Nordio
Mathai Joseph
Bertrand Meyer
Andrey Terekhov

Conference Organization

Conference Co-chairs

Andrey Terekhov	Saint Petersburg State University and Lanit-Tercom, Russia
Martin Nordio	ETH Zurich, Switzerland

Program Co-chairs

Mathai Joseph	Tata Consulting Services, India
Bertrand Meyer	ETH Zurich and Eiffel Software

Organization Chair

Iakov Kirilenko	Saint Petersburg State University and Lanit-Tercom, Russia

Publicity Chair

Nadia Polikarpova	ETH Zurich, Switzerland

Program Committee

Alberto Avritzer	Siemens, USA
Judith Bishop	Microsoft, USA
Manfred Broy	Technische Universität München, Germany
Bernd Bruegge	University of Munich, Germany
Lubomír Bulej	Charles University, Prague, Czech Republic
Jean Pierre Corriveau	Carleton University, Canada
Al Davis	University of Colorado and The Davis Company, USA
Barry Dwolatzky	Wits University, South Africa
Wolfgang Emmerich	University College London, UK
Gregor Engels	University of Paderborn, Germany
Victor Gergel	University of Nizhnyi Novgorod, Russia
Olly Gotel	Independent Researcher, New York City, USA
Nicolas Guelfi	University of Luxembourg, Luxembourg
Amar Gupta	University of Arizona, USA
Mike Hinchey	LERO, Ireland
Gerti Kappel	Vienna University of Technology, Austria

Vsevolod Kotlyarov	Saint Petersburg Polytechnical University, Russia
Vinay Kulkarni	Tata Research Development and Design Centre, India
Vidya Kulkarni	University of Delhi, India
Silvio Romero de Lemos Meira	Universidade Federal de Pernambuco, Brazil
Claudia Pons	University of La Plata, Argentina
Eduardo Santana de Almeida	Universidade Federal da Bahia (UFBA), Brazil
Anthony Savidis	Foundation for Research and Technology - Hellas (FORTH), Greece (Crete)
Anatoly Shalyto	St.-Petersburg State University of Information Technologies, Russia
Beijun Shen	Shanghai Jiao Tong University, China
Giordano Tamburrelli	Politecnico di Milano, Italy
Huynh quyet Thang	Hanoi University of Technology, Vietnam
Dang Van Hung	Vietnam National University, Vietnam

External Reviewers

Florian Schneider
Ita Richardson
Jonas Helming
Marco Zapletal
Maria Spichkova
Mario Gleirscher
Martina Seidl
Roman Mitin
Shareeful Islam

Table of Contents

A Smarter Way: The Software Engineering Method and Theory Initiative (Semat)

Ivar Jacobson

Ivar Jacobson International
ivar@ivarjacobson.com

Abstract. Semat and its large supporter base believes that software engineering is gravely hampered by immature practices. Specific problems include: The prevalence of fads more typical of the fashion industry than an engineering discipline, lack of a sound, widely accepted theoretical basis, a huge number of methods and method variants, with differences little understood and artificially magnified. SEMAT supports a process to refound software engineering based on a solid theory, proven principles and best practices that include; a kernel of widely-agreed elements, extensible for specific uses, addressing both technology and people issues. We focus on changing the way we deal with methods and processes, which will impact our industry, its education, its research and its developer community. Join this presentation on SEMAT by Ivar Jacobson to identify how we can change how we work today, as well as influence larger changes required to operate more successfully tomorrow.

1 Short Biography

Dr. Ivar Jacobson is a father of components and component architecture, use cases, the Unified Modeling Language and the Rational Unified Process. He has contributed to modern business modeling and aspect-oriented software development. However, all this is history. Lately he has been working on how to deal with methods and tools in a super-light and agile way. He has developed a practice concept that is now being adopted by both developers and tool vendors. Now he is one of the leaders of a worldwide network Semat, which has agreed to revolutionize software development.

He is also the principal author of six influential and best-selling books.

Ivar Jacobson is the chairman of Ivar Jacobson International which has subsidiaries in the US, UK, China, Singapore, Australia, Sweden and Canada.

M. Nordio et al. (Eds.): SEAFOOD 2010, LNBIP 54, p. 1, 2010.

The Consortium for IT Software Quality

Richard Mark Soley[1] and Bill Curtis[2]

[1] Object Management Group
[2] CAST Software

Rationale for CISQ—CISQ exists to address a significant challenge: the lack of visibility IT executives have into the quality and risk of their critical business applications. A fundamental assumption underlying CISQ is that global standards for measuring the attributes of software, especially at the source code level, are fundamental to meeting this challenge. The IT industry needs standard measures to support the use of quality attributes in benchmarking and controlling software acquisition. Currently software measures are too often manual, expensive, and based on inconsistent or even subjective definitions. In order to improve the discipline of application development CISQ has set four initial objectives presented in Table 1.

Table 1. CISQ Objectives

1	Raise international awareness of the critical challenge of IT software quality
2	Develop standard, automatable measures and anti-patterns for evaluating IT software quality
3	Promote global acceptance of the standard in acquiring IT software and services
4	Develop an infrastructure of authorized assessors and products using the standard

CISQ bases its mission, strategies, and tactics on the following premises:

- IT application quality is a critical business issue as more business processes are committed to software
- The current quality of IT application software exposes the business to unacceptable levels of risk and loss
- Businesses do not have governance structures sufficient to manage the risks to which poor quality application software exposes them
- Customers and providers of IT application software do not have a common basis for describing and managing the quality of delivered application software
- Business and government and their providers need a common voice to drive attention to and improvements in IT application software

CISQ will pursue the following measureable goals:

- 75% of the Global 1000 have an IT application software quality governance structure that involves the business
- 75% of Global 1000 use a common IT application software quality standard in contractual agreements with their suppliers/outsourcers
- 50% of the Global 1000 have established baselines and business value propositions for IT application software quality

M. Nordio et al. (Eds.): SEAFOOD 2010, LNBIP 54, pp. 2–5, 2010.

CISQ Products—To pursue its second objective, CISQ will form technical working groups for each of the high priority software attributes decided by the membership. CISQ technical working groups will define standard quality measures and software anti-patterns characterizing the software attributes of highest priority to CISQ members. Software anti-patterns represent vulnerabilities, weaknesses, and violations of good coding and architectural practice related to these high priority attributes. These working groups will produce four products described in Table 2 that will be submitted to the OMG standards process.

Table 2. CISQ Work Products

Product	Description	Availability
Software measures	Standard definitions at the source code level with tailoring guidelines for application to different languages and technologies	Repository
Software anti-patterns	Anti-patterns defined to a level that can be recognized in source code	Repository
Manipulation rules	Rules for aggregating software measures from the component to the application level and other guidelines as necessary for manipulating measures of software attributes	Document
Usage guidelines	Methods for adopting and using software attribute measures and anti-patterns in developing, acquiring, or benchmarking applications	Document

Based on the content of CISQ products, we anticipate that their final form will be of repositories of measures and anti-patterns that are maintained under configuration management. These measures and anti-patterns will be associated with rules and guidelines for adapting them to different languages, platforms, technologies, and uses. CISQ will also develop rules and guidelines for aggregated measures from the component to the application level.

CISQ-Related Standards—The most relevant existing standard is ISO 9126, now being replaced by ISO 25000, which describes a model of quality attributes. OMG supports several standards that CISQ will use to accelerate the development of standard measures of software attributes. These include the Knowledge Discovery Meta-Model which describes the elements resulting from a parse that provide the countable elements for quality metrics and the Structured Metrics Meta-model that provides a standard format for representing metrics. OMG is currently working on a standard for representing anti-patterns, vulnerabilities, weaknesses, and violations of good coding practice. CISQ will support the development and evolution of these standards.

CISQ Timetable—CISQ has initiated technical working groups in the first quarter of 2010 to begin work on measures for high priority software attributes. Initial measures will be available to CISQ members during 2011. It is anticipated that these measures will be certified via the OMG standards process during 2011. The schedule for establishing a repository of standard anti-patterns will follow the schedule for measures by two or more quarters since it will depend on the creation of a standard for representing anti-patterns.

CISQ Executive Forums—CISQ conducted two Executive Forums during the Fall of 2009, one in Frankfurt, Germany and one in Arlington, VA. A third Executive Forum will be conducted in Bangalore, India in June, 2010. The quality issues raised by the executives in attendance grouped into four categories; 1) specific quality attributes to be defined as quality measures in the CISQ standard, 2) primary uses for these quality measures, 3) support required for using quality measures effectively, and 4) methods for integrating quality measures into life cycle and acquisition processes. Participants wanted to prioritize the focus on application software, but did not want to artificially exclude system or embedded software. They prioritized five initial targets for CISQ for which CISQ has organized Technical Work Groups. Primary uses for the measures emerging from these groups included controlling internal development, managing the quality of externally supplied software, estimating maintenance effort/costs, managing application portfolios, and assessing business disruption risk.

Technical Work Groups—Five technical Work Groups have been formed to address four areas of measurement and the methods for using such measures. These groups are summarized in Table 3. Each group will have a technical leader selected from one of CISQ's member organizations. Work groups will launch their activities in an on-site meeting held during the first quarter of 2010. However, much of the work for each work group will be conducted virtually and coordinated by the work group leader.

Table 3. Technical Work Groups

Working group	Initial technical focus
Size	Develop a definition for automating Function Points
Maintainability	Measure factors affecting maintenance cost, effort, and duration
Reliability and Performance	Measure factors affecting availability and responsiveness to users
Security	Measure factors affecting vulnerability and leverage existing work in the assurance community
Best Practices	Define best practices for using code measures with internally and externally supplied software

Size—The initial objective of this group will be to create a definition of Function Points that is as close to IFPUG counting rules as possible, while resolving the issues necessary to enable fully automated counting at the source code level. Organizations participating in this work group will be encouraged to pilot the counting rules as they move through the standardization process. Possible future objectives will be to define functional measures for areas where current definitions may be weak such as Web interfaces or heavily algorithmic software.

Maintainability —This group will develop a definition of maintainability that is consistent with existing international standards, but sufficiently detailed to support automated counting at the source code level. In addition to a single summary measure characterizing maintainability, this group will develop measures of distinct factors that affect maintainability to provide better guidance for improving application quality. Finally this work group will develop rules for aggregating maintainability measures from the component to the application level.

Reliability and Performance—Since many common factors affect both reliability and performance, the measurement of these two quality attributes will be addressed in the same work group. This work group will be tasked with distinguishing which factors and anti-patterns affect both reliability and performance and which affect one but not the other. These results will be developed into source code measures and anti-patterns for each characteristic. Organizations participating in this work group will be encouraged to validate and calibrate these measures with operational criteria such as mean time to failure and user response time.

Security—This group will develop automated source code measures that predict the vulnerability of source code to external attack. This group will coordinate its work products with developments in the software assurance community such as the Common Weakness Enumeration and Common Vulnerability Scoring System. This work group will leverage the existing work accomplished by the software assurance community and the Software Assurance Task Force of OMG.

Best Practices—This group will define best practices for integrating quality attribute measures and anti-patterns into three types of processes; development and maintenance, acquisition of externally developed software, and application portfolio management. This group will define methods not only for using measures, but also for introducing, adopting, and supporting them. These best practices will supplement and extend guidelines in Practical Software Measurement and ISO 15939-Software Measurement Process for use with measures produced by static code analysis.

Reconciling Offshore Outsourcing with Model Based Testing

David Arnold[1], Jean-Pierre Corriveau[1], and Wei Shi[2]

[1] School of Computer Science, Carleton University, Ottawa, Canada
{darnold,jeanpier}@scs.carleton.ca
[2] Faculty of Business and IT, UOIT, Oshawa, Canada
wei.shi@uoit.ca

Abstract. In the context of offshore outsourcing, in order to validate the requirements of a stakeholder (the contractor) against the *actual* behavior of an implementation under test (IUT) developed by the contracted, it is necessary to have a requirement specification language from which test cases can be generated *and* executed on an *actual* IUT. Code-based testing tools are limited to unit testing and do not tackle validation *per se*. Conversely, model-based testing tools support the derivation of test cases from a requirements model. But such test cases are not necessarily executable and those tools that claim 'test execution' in fact offer *symbolic execution*, which is carried out using a model of the IUT, *not* the actual IUT. Here, we overview a requirements specification language and its corresponding fully implemented framework, that support the validation of IUT-independent requirements against actual IUT behavior, as required by offshore outsourcing.

Keywords: validation, requirements specification, model-based testing, scenarios, test case generation, executable test cases, contracts.

1 Introduction

In the context of software offshore outsourcing, Meyer [1] observes, "quality is indeed the central issue". A quality-driven approach to software development and testing demands that, ultimately, the requirements of stakeholders be *validated* against the *actual behavior* of an implementation under test (IUT). This is particularly true in the context of software offshore outsourcing. Let us elaborate. As argued elsewhere [2], we view outsourcing as a business relationship and thus assume that a *contract* is required in order to define a) what services are requested from the *contracted* party and b) how these services are to be delivered to the satisfaction of the *contractor*. More precisely, a software offshore outsourcing contract must include, among its quality assurance facets, the specification of a systematic (ideally *objective* and *automated*) approach to the validation of the requirements of the stakeholder (i.e., the contractor) against the *actual behavior* of an implementation under test (IUT) delivered by the contracted.

Unfortunately, typically, there is no such contract, and no systematic and automated approach to validation. Quite on the contrary, generally, the contracted is assumed to

M. Nordio et al. (Eds.): SEAFOOD 2010, LNBIP 54, pp. 6–22, 2010.

mostly carry out extensive unit testing [3]. Depending on the scope of the project, integration testing [3] may also be completely left to the contracted, or, involve both the contractor and the contracted in projects in which the outsourced software is merely a component of a larger system. In parallel to such low-level testing, extensive quality assurance activities may take place. The latter involve gathering metrics pertaining to code coverage, test suite coverage, frequency of build errors and of their resolution time, bug frequency and resolution time, etc. But neither unit/integration testing, nor metrics, tackle the problem we focus on in this paper, namely the *automated* validation of the requirements of the contractor against the *actual behavior* of an IUT delivered by the contracted. In fact, in the context of outsourcing, current practice with respect to validation often consists in offloading it to a separate group of testers. That is, generally, system-level validation is not performed by the developers, nor by the clients (i.e., the stakeholders). Instead, it is left to a separate team of testers, which will treat the IUT as a black box and merely verify that 'representative' use-cases [3] are handled correctly (in terms of system inputs and outputs). In the context of offshore outsourcing, such an approach leads to two observations: First, a separate team of testers entails one more participant in the already complex communication puzzle inherent to offshore outsourcing. Second, regardless of whether such testers report to the contracted, or work for the contractor, it is crucial that the contractor and the contracted agree *a priori* (ideally via a contract taking the form of a testable requirements model [2]) on what constitutes successful validation.

In this paper, we do not focus on organizational or process aspects of validation[1]. Instead, we present a tool that does support the *automated* validation of the requirements of the contractor against the *actual behavior* of an IUT delivered by the contracted. This is achieved via the automatic generation of executable test cases from a testable IUT-independent model of the requirements.

Before introducing our proposal, it is important to remark that modeling tools are mainly used to create models of (some aspects of) an IUT. Such tools provide support for model specification, analysis, and maintenance. While requirements can be modeled within (e.g., as use cases in the UML), and even possibly semantically linked to other models supported by, such tools, the latter generally do not have the ability to generate test cases, let alone run and monitor them against an actual (even possibly generated) IUT. Consequently, such modeling tools are not relevant to this paper, as they do not tackle the specific kind of validation we address.

Similarly, a *test automation framework* does not support validation *per se*. Such a framework generally accepts executable test cases that *already* have been manually created, automatically generated, or pre-recorded. The automation framework then executes the test sequences without human interaction. With respect to validation, such frameworks present at least two specific problems: First, requirements are not captured anywhere (but instead embedded implicitly in test cases) and thus traceability between requirements and test cases is inexistent. Second, test cases in such

[1] We insist however that any "state-of-the-art development process" and "vendor management practice" that does not *explicitly* tackle the automated validation of the requirements of the contractor against the actual behavior of an IUT is, from our viewpoint, inadequate in the context of offshore outsourcing [2]. In other words, we place this very specific kind of validation at the heart of offshore outsourcing.

frameworks are generally limited to unit testing (i.e., testing of procedures [3]) and very simple scenario testing [3] (e.g., exercising a graphical user interface). Semantically, the expression of requirements for industrial software systems is far more complex [4]. Consequently, we will not discuss further such frameworks.

Also, we must emphasize that, in the context of this paper, testing notations *in vacuo* are of no interest. For example, TTCN-3 (the Tree and Tabular Combined Notation) [5] is an international standard that is widely used to capture functional test cases. But its syntax and semantics are of little importance here: TTCN is purely descriptive and offers no operational semantics *per se*. Similarly, the UML's use cases and interaction diagrams [3] are *modeling* notations used to capture scenarios. Capturing a scenario can be semantically challenging [6] yet remains a much simpler task than building a tool capable of setting up this scenario in an IUT, monitoring its multiple (possibly concurrent) executions at run time, and reporting on the outcomes of the later! In the same vein, we remark that the UML's Object Constraint Language (OCL) does not support semantically the notion of a scenario and that, consequently, the few tools capable of generating executable test cases from OCL statements generally have such test cases limited to the scope of a class[2].

Not surprisingly, given the previous observations, Grieskamp [4] from Microsoft Research, comments that current testing practices are not only laborious and expensive but often unsystematic, lacking methodology and adequate tool support.

Current approaches to validation and testing fall into two categories: code-centric and model-centric. A code-centric approach to validation and testing, such as Test-Driven Design (TDD) [7], typically uses *test cases* (as opposed to more abstract *tests* [3][3]) written at the implementation level in order to guide development. A TDD approach begins by creating a test case addressing one or more requirements of a software system being developed. The test case is executed against this system, usually resulting in a failure. Code is then added to the system until this test case succeeds. The process repeats until all relevant requirements have been satisfied, but there is little effort to scope and capture such requirements in a model! Test cases are purely implementation-driven and implementation-specific (as opposed to proceeding from the requirements of stakeholders): validation *per se* is not addressed [8].

Model-Based Testing (MBT) involves the derivation of tests from a model that describes some aspects of an IUT. More precisely, an MBT tool uses various algorithms and strategies to generate tests from a behavioral model of the IUT. Such a model is usually a partial representation of the IUT's behavior, 'partial' because the model abstracts away some of the implementation details. Tests derived from such a model are functional ones expressed at the same level of abstraction as the model. Such tests can then grouped together to form an abstract test suite. Such an abstract test suite *cannot* be directly executed against an IUT because the tests are not at the same level of abstraction as the code. In general, such tools use a Finite State Machine (FSM) or FSM-like representation to create a behavioral model of the IUT. The model is then traversed

[2] In fact, in OCL, constraints can be associated not only with a class's attributes and operations, but also with use cases, interaction diagrams, etc. However, currently, test case generation from OCL statements is limited to class scope and requires that such statements be first embedded in a specific implementation (an approach quite far from the model-based derivation and execution of test cases we aim for).

[3] A test case can in fact be viewed as an *instantiation* of a test for a specific IUT [3].

according to some test 'purposes' [3] in order to generate test cases. Several MBT tools claim to offer test case generation and execution. But it is important to understand that such 'execution' typically consists in *symbolic execution*, that is, is carried out using a (typically state-based) *model* of the IUT, *not* the actual IUT. The latter (which is taken to be a black-box binary) is merely to be stimulated in order for it to generate the outputs that act as triggers for the transitions of this state-based model.

Most interestingly, a survey of existing MBT tools [8] reveals that there are significant semantic differences between the specification languages used in such tools. For example, one can contrast the "business-readable (i.e., stakeholder-friendly)" specification language of Cucumber [9], which is utterly simplistic, with the semantic richness of Spec# [10] and the subtle complexities of expressing intricate scenario interrelationships [6]. Indeed, in our opinion, Spec Explorer [11] constitutes the state-of-art in MBT tools because Spec#, its specification language, is able to capture a detailed model of an IUT's behavior, which can be exercised via the symbolic execution of user-specified scenarios. Spec# is a textual programming language that includes and extends C#. In addition to the functionality provided by C#, Spec# adds pre- and post-conditions [12], high-level data types, logical quantifiers (e.g., *forAll* and *Exists*), and a simple form of scenarios (which is generally absent in other state-based approaches). Thus, a Spec# model can be viewed as a program. But, as with most other existing MBT approaches, even in Spec Explorer requirements are *not* tested against an actual IUT, but rather against a *model* of the behavior of this IUT. More precisely, the *executability* of test cases is defined with respect to a state-based model and is rooted in the concept of state exploration (which faces the difficult problem of state explosion [4, 11]).

Ultimately if existing MBT tools are to tackle the validation of the requirements of the stakeholder (i.e., the contractor) against the *actual behavior* of an IUT delivered by the contracted, then the generated test cases must be 'transformed' into an executable test suite that can run against an IUT. Such a transformation is performed via the use of 'glue code'. That is, test cases obtained from a model are subsequently coded, typically manually. The resulting code (which includes not only executable test cases but also test drivers and oracles [3]) must be *handcrafted* and may end up *not* corresponding to the model-derived test cases. Moreover, this glue code is implementation-specific: both its reusability across several IUTs and its maintainability are highly problematic [13]. In other words, the creation of glue code is a non-automated endeavor that is time-consuming and just as error-prone as the development of the original IUT. Consequently, in the context of offshore outsourcing, the use of glue code is likely to greatly hinder the ability to carry out validation in a systematic, ideally automated way.

In the rest of this paper, we overview the specification language and the fully implemented framework we have built to support the validation approach we believe is required by offshore outsourcing.

2 An Alternative Approach to MBT

2.1 Semantic Foundations

In order to validate the requirements of a stakeholder (the contractor) against the actual behavior of a candidate IUT submitted by the contracted, it is necessary to have a specification language from which test cases can be generated *and* executed on an actual IUT (as opposed to a model of the latter). This position statement leads to three questions that we will address in the rest of this section: First, what are to be the semantics of this specification language? Second, how is traceability between a model expressed in this language and an IUT to be specified and maintained? And, third, how are test cases to be generated and executed against an IUT?

With respect to semantics, Spec# [10] aims at reducing the gap between the specification language and an implementation language in order to improve correspondence between model and IUT. While Spec# can be easily picked up by someone with C# programming experience, in the context of validation, it is difficult for a stakeholder to understand it, as it resides at a low-level of abstraction. Yet it is desirable to offer an *IUT-independent* specification language that stakeholders can master. For offshore outsourcing, this is particularly true when considering that, in addition to the contractor, it is often the case that stakeholders will include the separate team of testers mentioned earlier. Much like the contractor, such testers want to treat the IUT as a black box whose behavior is to be used to validate the *IUT-independent* requirements.

On the topic of semantics, Grieskamp's [4] observes that industrial users of MBT approaches prefer scenario-based (as opposed to state-based) semantics for the specification language of an MBT tool. Consequently, we have rooted the semantics of our proposed approach to MBT in the notions of *responsibilities* and *scenarios* [6, 14]: scenarios are conceptualized as grammars of responsibilities [14]. Each responsibility represents a simple action or task. Intuitively, a responsibility is either to be bound to a procedure within an IUT, or the responsibility is to be decomposed into a sub-grammar of responsibilities (as illustrated later). In addition to responsibilities and scenarios, our semantics offer a set of *Design-by-Contract* [12] elements such as pre- and post- conditions, and invariants (which have been shown to be very useful for unit testing [15] and which will be illustrated in the next section).

Our proposed specification language (called ACL for Another Contract Language), which is to be used to model IUT-independent requirements, is not limited to functional dynamic testing (in contrast to AutoTest [15] and similar tools): it also supports static testing, as well as the evaluation of metrics (as explained shortly).

Most importantly, in contrast to existing MBT approaches and tools, we root validation not only in the generation of IUT-independent tests but also in the execution of the *corresponding* test cases on an *actual* IUT (not a model of it). In the context of offshore outsourcing, this decision is crucial. Let us elaborate. Outsourcing is often motivated by cost reduction considerations. The use of any specification language to obtain a requirements model represents a significant investment of time and money. This investment is leveraged if the requirements model is IUT-independent: only in this case will changes to the IUT *not* entail changes to the requirements model. (In fact, an IUT-independent model can be reused across a set of candidate IUTs.) For the same reason, we aim for IUT-independent tests (which are thus non-executable on an IUT). If symbolic execution is then used, the specific test cases generated from the IUT-independent tests will be executed on a behavioral model of the IUT. But an outsourcing contract [2] will *not* be concerned with validation against a behavioral model of an IUT, but rather against the actual behavior of an actual IUT! And without such validation, in our opinion, there is very little possibility of formalizing an outsourcing contract.

Insisting on the executability of test cases against an actual IUT requires that we now address how such test cases can be derived from IUT-independent tests, themselves generated from an IUT-independent requirements model. An answer requires a) a transformation from such generated tests to test cases executable on a particular IUT and b) the instrumentation of such executable test cases, that is, the addition to the IUT of run-time monitoring code in order to observe/evaluate the outcomes of the executable test cases. As previously mentioned, a manual transformation from IUT-independent tests to test cases executable on an IUT is undesirable: it is not only time-consuming but often error-prone, and the resulting executable test cases may not correspond to the tests generated from the requirements model. Thus, we advocate an automated transformation, as well as automatic instrumentation of the IUT. This has a crucial consequence for the semantics of ACL: our position is that *only* semantics that enable their automated transformation to IUT-executable test cases and automatic instrumentation are to be included in ACL.

The question then is: how does such transformation and instrumentation work? The answer requires that we introduce the validation framework (VF) we have developed.

2.2 Using the Validation Framework

Our VF [16] operates on three input elements. The first element is the Testable Requirements Model (hereafter TRM). This model is expressed in ACL, a high-level general-purpose requirements *contract* language. We use here the word 'contract' because a TRM is formed of a set of contracts, as will be illustrated in the next section. ACL is closely tied to requirements by defining constructs for the representation of scenarios, and design-by-contract constructs [12]. Additional domain-specific constructs can also be added to the ACL, via modules known as *plug-ins* (as explained elsewhere [16]). The second input element is the candidate IUT against which the TRM will be executed. Currently, this IUT is a .NET executable (for which we do not require the source code). *Bindings* represent the third and final input element required by the VF. Before a TRM can be executed, the types, responsibilities, and *observability* [3] requirements of the TRM must be bound to concrete implementation artifacts located within the IUT. A structural representation of the IUT is first obtained automatically. Our binding tool, which is part of the VF, uses this structural representation to map elements from the TRM to types and procedures defined within the candidate IUT. Most importantly, our binding tool is able to automatically infer most of the bindings required between a TRM and an IUT [13]. Such bindings are crucial for three reasons. First, they allow the TRM to be independent of implementation details, as specific type and procedure names used with the candidate IUT *do not* have to exist within the TRM. Second, because each IUT has its own bindings to a TRM, several candidate IUTs can be tested against a single TRM. Finally, bindings provide explicit traceability between a TRM and IUT.

Users of our VF can bind contract elements to procedures and types of the IUT manually, or use the Automated Binding Engine (ABE) we provide. ABE supports an open approach to the automation of binding creation: different algorithms for finding bindings are separately implemented in different *binding modules*. We have implemented two such binding modules as part of the current release of our VF [16]. The first binding module takes into account the names of types and procedures in order to find matches, whereas the second module uses only structural information such as return type and parameter type/ordering to infer a binding. Each of our two implemented binding modules have correctly bound approximately 95% of the required bindings found in the five case studies we have developed so far (approx. 200 bindings) [16]. Missing bindings are specified manually.

ACL provides the user of our VF with built-in (and user-defined) static checks, dynamic checks, and metric evaluators. (The Container ACL model found in [16] provides a simple example that includes static and dynamic checks, as well as metric evaluators.) A static check performs a check on the structure of an IUT. Such check is accomplished without execution. Examples of currently supported static checks include checks involving inheritance (e.g., type A must be a descendant of type B), and checks on types (e.g., type A must contain a variable of type B). A static check can be viewed as an operation: each check has a return type and may accept a fixed number of parameters. All static checks are guaranteed to be side effect free. The point is that should a contractor have requirements pertaining to the structure of an IUT, our proposed tool is able to validate such requirements.

A dynamic check is used to perform a check on the IUT during execution. That is, a dynamic check can only be evaluated while the IUT is being executed. The evaluation of pre- and post-conditions, and of invariants constitutes one category of dynamic checks, particularly relevant to unit testing. Other examples of dynamic checks include: testing the value of a variable at a given point, ensuring a given state exists within an object (with respect to the values of that object's instance variables), and validating data sent between two different objects. As with static checks, dynamic checks can be viewed as an operation with a return type and parameter set. The execution of a dynamic check is also guaranteed to be side effect free.

Metric evaluators are used to analyze and report on the metrics gathered while the candidate IUT was executing. Metric gathering is automatically performed by the VF. Once metric gathering is complete and the IUT has concluded execution, the metric evaluators are invoked. Examples of a metric evaluator include: performance, space, and network use analysis. Metric evaluators are side effect free. Most importantly, they allow our proposed tool to tackle the validation of non-functional requirements, something that is essentially downplayed in most existing approaches and tools for MBT. In fact, to the best of our knowledge, very few, if any, MBT tool, except ours, addresses both (static and dynamic) functional *and* non-functional requirements (via metric evaluators) within the same specification language. As a matter of fact, ACL offers a semantic richness (static and dynamic testing, responsibilities and scenarios, metric evaluators) that enables the contractor to develop a requirements model (to be included in the outsourcing contract) that can address system-level behavior of an IUT, *as well as* scenario and unit testing, static analysis and non-functional requirements. We believe this is absolutely necessary if indeed ACL is to offer the semantic flexibility (i.e., high- *and* low-level semantics) that industrial outsourcing projects require [4].

Once the TRM has been specified and bound to a candidate IUT, the TRM is compiled. Upon a successful compilation, all elements of the TRM have been bound to IUT artifacts and any required plug-ins have been located and initialized. The result of such a compilation is a single file that contains all information required to execute the TRM against a candidate IUT. (Details lie beyond the scope of this paper.) The validation of a Testable Requirements Model (TRM) begins with a structural analysis of the candidate IUT, and with execution of any static checks. Following execution of the static checks, the VF executes the IUT. The VF is able to track and record the execution paths generated by the IUT, as well as execute any dynamic checks, and gather metrics indicated by the TRM. The execution paths are used to determine if each scenario execution *matches* the grammar of responsibilities corresponding to it within the TRM (see next section). Next, metric evaluators are used to analyze and interpret any metric data that was gathered during execution of the IUT. All of the results generated from execution of the TRM against the candidate IUT are written to a Contract Evaluation Report (CER). The generation of the CER completes the process of executing a TRM against a candidate IUT. The CER indicates where the candidate IUT matches the TRM, and where any deviations from the TRM were observed. For example, when a pre- or post-condition fails, the execution proceeds but that failure is logged in the CER. Also, when a scenario is executed by an IUT, the specified grammar of responsibilities must hold in order for the scenario to be considered to have succeeded. That is, for success, the responsibilities that compose the scenario must be executed in an order that satisfies the grammar. If the scenario cannot be executed, or responsibilities/events that are not defined by the scenario are executed, then the scenario is deemed to have failed. This mismatch is also reported in the CER. Several quality control and analysis methods could then be used to analyze the generated CER and apply their findings to the software development process, or calculate information important to management and other stakeholders. Such methods currently lie beyond the scope of our work.

The key point of this overview is that once a TRM is bound to an IUT, all dynamic checks and metrics evaluators are automatically instrumented in the IUT whose execution is also controlled by the VF (e.g., in order to monitor scenario instance creation and matching). In order to discuss scenario testing, we must first illustrate the semantics of the language we use to specify a TRM, especially those features that pertain to unit and scenario testing.

3 A Partial Example

We now present excerpts of a medium-size case study that deals with how students register in their courses at a university and how they obtain grades for these courses. Our intent is not to motivate the contracts used, nor to explain at length how this example is processed. Instead, we aim at providing the reader with a substantial (i.e., non-trivial) example in order to a) illustrate the semantics of ACL, especially pertaining to scenarios and b) subsequently discuss the basics of unit and scenario testing in the VF. (The complete example is in [16] and is 49 pages long. Most importantly it does compile and run.)

We use the // and /* */ to provide comments directly in the example, as this facilitates presenting explanations in the ACL rather than after it.

The Course contract represents a single university course. A course is created by the university, and consists of a name, code, a list of prerequisites, a list of students currently enrolled in the course, and a size limit on the number of students that can take the course.

```
Namespace Examples.School{
Contract Course {
/* Once the contract Course is bound to a type of the IUT, each time an instance of
this type is created, a new instance of contract Course is associated with it. A contract
can be bound to several types.
   Parameters are values supplied to a contract. These values can be provided either
via other contracts (i.e., statically), or at binding time (in which case all instances of
the class bound to this contract will share the same parameter values). Finally,
parameter values can be left unspecified until run-time, using the keyword
InstanceBind, in which case, each time an instance of a class bound to this contract is
created, the VF will prompt the user for all required parameter values. These three
options are extremely important in dealing with test case generation, as explained
later. */

Parameters
{ Scalar Boolean EnforcePreRequisites = { true, default false };
  [0-2] Scalar Integer InstanceBind NumMidterms = 1;
  [0-5] Scalar Integer InstanceBind NumAssignments = 1;
 Scalar Boolean InstanceBind HasFinal = { default true, false };          }

/* An observability is a query-method that is used to provide state information about
the IUT to the TRM. That is, they are read-only methods that acquire and return a
value stored by the IUT. */
Observability String Name();
Observability Integer Code();
/* The VF supports scalars (one value) and Lists (set of values).
Other observabilities skipped here include a list of students, a cap size, a list of
prerequisites, the weight for assignments, etc. We now look at some more of these: */

//example of an observability with a parameter
Observability Integer  MarkForStudent(tStudent student);
// example of statically setting a parameter
Observability Boolean HasFinal()    { Parameters.HasFinal == true; }

/* The responsibilities new and finalize are special:
The body of the new responsibility is executed immediately following the creation of
a new contract instance.    It only can use post-conditions        */
Responsibility new()
{  Post(Name() not= null); Post(Code() not= 0);
   Post(Students().Length() == 0); Post(TotalMarks() == 100); }
/* The body of the finalize responsibility is executed immediately before the
destruction of the current contract  instance.    */
Responsibility finalize()  { Pre(Students().Length() == 0);  }

/* Invariants provide a way to specify a set of checks that are to be executed before
and after the execution of all bound responsibilities. Invariants precede pre-conditions
and follow post-conditions.            */
Invariant IsFullCheck {  Students().Length() <= CapSize(); }
```

```
/* A stub is a choice point where one of several possible responsibilities is selected
based on some criterion. Here, we use the value of a parameter to choose.  */
stub Responsibility AddStudent(tStudent s)
{ [Default] AddStudentNoPreReqCheck(s);
  [Parameters.EnforcePreRequisites == true]  AddStudentPreReqCheck(s);   }

/* Here is a simple responsibility, which will be used if prerequisites are set to not be
enforced (via the parameter). It just checks that the student is not already in the
course. The keyword Execute indicates where execution occurs. */
Responsibility AddStudentNoPreReqCheck(tStudent s)
{  Pre(Students().Contains(s) == false);  Execute();
   Post(Students().Contains(s) == true);   }
/* Other responsibilities include AddStudentPreReqCheck and RemoveStudent. */

// a scenario defines a grammar of responsibilities
Scenario ReportMarks
{ Trigger(observe(TermEnded)),     //it must be triggered by an event (a symbol)
/* Each time a scenario's trigger is satisfied, it creates a new scenario instance (of
itself). Instances of contracts can be referenced by other contracts.
Semantically, this is a powerful mechanism of our VF. Here, the example is simple
because there's only 1 instance of the contract for the university. A complex
example, which involves the keyword bindpoint will be presented later in this section.
The keyword once states that the variable does not change once its value is set. */
once Scalar Contract University u = instance;

/* The body of the each statement contains a single grammar element. It captures that
the fact that ReportMark responsibility (defined in the university contract instance u)
must be invoked using our course and the current student (denoted by the iterator
keyword) and that the mark reported by the MarkForStudent() observability method
is provided. The purpose of this element is to ensure that the correct mark for the
given student is recorded.
each(Students()) {u.ReportMark(context, iterator, MarkForStudent(iterator))},
/* The ',' operator is the 'follows' operator above.

The scenario is completed with a termination condition. A scenario's termination
condition is used to specify when the scenario is complete.   */
Terminate(fire(MarksRecorded));    }
/* The Exports section defines the IUT binding points required for the contract, and
also includes any binding constraints. Our Course contract only requires a single
binding point: tStudent. The binding point begins with the Type keyword to denote
that the binding of the tStudent symbol is to be made against a type within the IUT.
   The conforms keyword is used to indicate that the IUT type that the tStudent sym-
bol is bound to will automatically have the Student contract applied to it. The tStu-
dent binding point contains a single binding rule that states that the IUT type that is
bound to the tStudent symbol must be the same type that is bound to the tStudent
symbol found within the University contract.  */
```

```
Exports
{ Type tStudent conforms Student { University::tStudent; }
}}} //end of Course contract

/*The ProjectCourse contract represents a refinement of the Course contract. It is
used for courses that also include a course project.*/
Namespace Examples.School
{ Contract ProjectCourse extends Course {
/* contracts can be organized hierarchically using the extends keyword. Usual rules
for how to deal with pre- and post-conditions [12] apply. */
Parameters
{ Scalar Boolean InstanceBind HasProject = { default true, false };
//the rest of the contract is not relevant to this paper
} //end of ProjectCourse contract

/* The Student contract represents an individual student enrolled at a university. */
Namespace Examples.School {
Contract Student {
Observability List Integer CompletedCourses();
/* scalar (failures) and observabilities (CurrentCourses, StudentNumber, Name,
IsFullTime ) are then defined, as well as responsibilities: SelectCourse (which
returns a course), RegisterCourse , DropCourse, RegisterCourse, DoAssignment,
DoMidterm, DoProject and DoFinal.
We now look at stub DoAssignment. The rationale for using a stub is that is if a stu-
dent is not taking a course that has any assignments, then the student will not require a
corresponding responsibility (which is declared after the definition of the stub of the
same name). The body of the DoAssignment responsibility stub begins with the ex-
traction of the Course contract instance from the provided IUT instance representing
the given course that we are doing the assignment for. This is achieved using the
keyword bindpoint. Note that if the resultant contract type does not match the de-
clared type, a run-time error will be issued.
   It is important to note that stubs are not bound but instead reduced to a responsibil-
ity (which is then bound). So there is no ambiguity between the stub and the responsi-
bility DoAssignment, despite using the same name.*/
stub Responsibility DoAssignment(tCourse c)
{ Contract Course course = c.bindpoint;
 [course.Parameters.NumAssignments > 0] DoAssignment(c); }
Responsibility DoAssignment(tCourse c);

/* The DoProject() responsibility is an example of a responsibility that is not bound to
a corresponding IUT procedure, but rather is specified as a grammar of other respon-
sibilities and events. This illustrates another use of events, beyond triggers and termi-
nations of scenarios. Events exist at run-time in the space of execution of the TRM, as
opposed to the one of the IUT. The run-time space of the TRM maintains all relevant
contract information, including contract and scenario instances.*/
Responsibility DoProject(tCourse c)
{       FormATeam(c), observe(TeamFinalized), WorkOnProject(c);    }
```

```
/* We include the two scenarios of this contract to illustrate the semantic complexity
our VF can currently handle. The keyword atomic defines a grammar of
responsibilities such that no other responsibilities of this contract instance are allowed
to execute except the ones specified within the grammar. Due to space limitations, we
leave it to the reader to either figure out the details or read them elsewhere [16]. */
Scenario RegisterForCourses {
Scalar tCourse course;     Contract University u = instance;
Trigger(observe(CoursesCreated), IsCreated()),
/*triggered IF courses have been created and the student is also created (isCreated is a
responsibility in this contract) */
 choice(IsFullTime()) true
  { ( atomic
     { course = SelectCourse(u.Courses()),
       //via bindpoint get the instance for the selected course
       choice(course.bindpoint.IsFull()) true
         { course = SelectCourse(u.Courses()), redo}  }, //until a course is not full
   // keyword context refers to the current contract instance
     u.RegisterStudentForCourse(context, course),
     RegisterCourse(course)
    ) [0-u.Parameters.MaxCoursesForFTStudents] //repeat atomic
  }
   alternative(false) //student is part-time (PT)
   { ( atomic
      {  course = SelectCourse(u.Courses()),
         choice(course.bindpoint.IsFull()) true
          { course = SelectCourse(u.Courses()), redo   }},
      u.RegisterStudentForCourse(context, course),
      RegisterCourse(course)
      )[0-u.Parameters.MaxCoursesForPTStudents] },
Terminate();  } //end of scenario RegisterForCourses

Scenario TakeCourses {
failures = 0; //number of failures in the current term
Trigger(observe(TermStarted)),
parallel
{ // for all courses of that term
  Contract Course course = instance;
  //if and only if that course is one taken by this student
  Check(CurrentCourses().Contains(course.bindpoint));
  atomic
   { (parallel//can do assignmnts, midterm, proj concurrently
       { (DoAssignment(course.bindpoint))
         [course.Parameters.NumAssignments]  }
      | //use OR, not AND, to avoid ordering
         (DoMidterm(course.bindpoint))
          [course.Parameters.NumMidterms]
      |
```

```
            (DoProject(course.bindpoint))
            [course sameas ProjectCourse &&
                course.Parameters.HasProject]
        ),
        (DoFinal(course.bindpoint)
          [course.Parameters.HasFinal]
          }
      alternative( not observe(LastDayToDrop))
        { DropCourse(course.bindpoint) }
}[CurrentCourses().Length()];
Terminate();  } //end of scenario TakeCourses

/* We omit most of the University contract, which does not add to this presentation.
We mostly focus below on its main scenario, which pertains to modeling a term. */

MainContract University
 {Parameters
     { [1-100] Scalar Integer InstanceBind UniversityCourses;
      Scalar Integer MaxCoursesForFTStudents = 4;
      Scalar Integer MaxCoursesForPTStudents = 2;
      Scalar Integer PassRate = 70;   }
/* several observabilities, responsibilities and some scenarios are omitted.  */

Responsibility ReportMark     (tCourse course, tStudent student, Integer mark)
/* The course, the student and the mark to be recorded are provided as parameters.
Each parameter of the responsibility is bound to a parameter of the procedure bound
to this responsibility. */
   {  choice(mark) < Parameters.PassRate   // the number of failures is recorded
           {  student.bindpoint.failures = student.bindpoint.failures + 1;  }  }
Scenario CreateCourses
     { Trigger(new()),
/* all courses of the term, in Parameters.UniversityCourses, must be created */
       CreateCourse(dontcare, dontcare) [Parameters.UniversityCourses],
        Terminate(fire(CoursesCreated));   }
Scenario CreateStudents
     { Trigger(new()), CreateStudent(dontcare)+, Terminate(finalize());   }

Scenario Term
/* term management via doing responsibilities in a particular order and firing the
corresponding events  */
     { Trigger(new()),
      ( CreateCourse()[Parameters.UniversityCourses],
        TermStarted(), fire(TermStarted), LastDayToDrop(), fire(LastDayToDrop),
       TermEnded(), fire(TermEnded), observe(MarksRecorded)
                [Parameters.UniversityCourses],
        CalculatePassFail(), DestroyCourse()[Parameters.UniversityCourses],
```

```
        fire(TermComplete)
      )+,
      Terminate(finalize());
  }
```
/* We conclude with an example of inter-scenario relationships [6]. Whereas a scenario instance is tied to a contract instance (its 'owner'), relations are not. This complicates their monitoring: each time a scenario instance is created or terminates, *all* relations referring to this scenario must be verified for compliance. */

```
Interaction School
{ Relation Creation // creation of students and courses can be in any order
    { Contract University u; (u.CreateStudents || u.CreateCourses); }
  Relation Cancelling
```
/* for any course created by the university, cancelling it is optional until the term starts. The keyword *dontcare* is used to ignore the name and code of the courses. The use of dontcare simplifies test case generation!! */

```
    { Contract University u; Instance c; //The VF figures out c is of type tCourse
      c = u.CreateCourse(dontcare, dontcare), (u.CancelCourse(c))?,
      observe(TermStarted);    } }   //other relations are omitted
} of Interaction School
```

4 Scenario Testing

In this section, we mainly focus on how scenarios expressed in ACL can be validated against the actual behavior of an IUT. For simplicity, hereafter, the term 'scenario' will refer to all forms of grammars of responsibilities in ACL (namely, responsibilities such as ***DoProject***, as well as scenarios and relations).

First, as explained earlier, the TRM will be bound to an IUT and compiled. Its dynamic checks (and metric evaluators) will be automatically instrumented in the selected IUT. Then testing proper begins. Static checks will be verified and their outcomes logged. Then the VF runs the IUT. Recall that the VF is able to track and record the execution paths generated by the IUT, as well as execute any dynamic checks, and gather metrics indicated by the TRM. Such execution paths are automatically *matched* against the scenarios of the TRM. Conceptually this task is not complex. Its implementation, however, is not trivial: the VF must monitor/stop/restart the execution of procedures of the IUT, as well as keep track of all contract and scenario instance creation and termination, and all events. (Details are given in [16].)

Second, the VF must tackle test case generation. The simplest strategy consists in *not* generating any tests from the TRM and instead leaving the creator of the IUT to supply a test suite. In this case, the TRM captures what is valid and what is not, and the VF provides automatic instrumentation, as well as run-time monitoring and logging of scenario satisfaction or failure. With this strategy, it is entirely left to the IUT-provider to code a test suite that defines a space of executions of the IUT in which these contracts/scenarios are validated. The difficulty with this approach is that the issue of *coverage* [3] of the TRM is completely hidden from the creators of the TRM (i.e., stakeholders such as the contractor and/or the testers), which is problematic! In our opinion, stakeholders must have a say in 'how much' a TRM is to be tested [2].

Coverage at the level of unit testing is considerably simpler than for scenarios. It rests on the use of well-known combinatorial techniques (chapter 6 in [3]) to address, for example, the coverage of the Boolean clauses of pre- and post-conditions. Also, as with AutoTest [15], instances can be automatically created with random states (that must satisfy the relevant invariants). Alternatively, the variables needed to (possibly partially) set the state of an instance under test (e.g., whether or not a student is full-time) can be defined statically, or when binding the TRM to an IUT, or at run-time (e.g., via the use of the *InstanceBind* keyword).

For scenario testing, the key idea is that scenarios are *grammars* and that, as with state machines, there are well-known algorithms to obtain a selection of paths through a grammar according to some coverage criterion [2]. Indeed, this idea has already been used in several distinct approaches to test case generation from scenarios [e.g., 17, 18]. Here, we only need to know that a test case consists of a specific path through a scenario, as well as the data (called *path sensitization data* [2, 3]) that enables this path to be taken.

Consider, for example, scenario ***RegisterForCourses*** in our example. A test case **TC1** through this scenario could be that a part-time student selects a first course which is full, then selects two that are not (and thus, for which registration proceeds). The question then is: how can this test case be generated *and* executed by our VF?

With respect to test case generation, the process starts by having the VF produce an internal representation of each scenario to test as a control flow graph [3]. Then, for each such graph, the user of the VF selects a coverage criterion. At this point in time, the VF offers “all-statements” and “all-branches” coverage [3, 18]. Each coverage criterion is associated with a traversal algorithm that generates a test suite sufficient to cover the graph at hand. Binder [3] discusses at length such algorithms (e.g., how conditional statements and loops are covered), which are also at the basis of similar approaches (e.g., [17, 18]). From this viewpoint, a test case can be thought of as a particular path of execution through a scenario. For example, for **TC1**:

```
{  (observe (CoursesCreated) == true), (context.IsCreated() == true),
   (context.IsFullTime() == false) ,
   (assign (course)) , (course.bindpoint.IsFull() ==  true)
   (assign (course)), (course.bindpoint.IsFull() ==  false)
   u.RegisterStudentForCourse(context, course),
   RegisterCourse(course),
   (assign (course)), (course.bindpoint.IsFull() ==  false)
   u.RegisterStudentForCourse(context, course),
   RegisterCourse(course),          Terminate() }
```

This path corresponds to the following specific branching decisions: the event *CoursesCreated* has been fired, the contract instance at hand (i.e., the *context*, which is a student) is created (i.e., student number is not 0) and is not full time, the first course attempted is full, the second is not, the atomic block is to execute twice, the third course attempted is not full.

It is crucial to understand that such a path is *not* executable: we need actual instances (i.e., a student, a university, and three courses). And such instances must typically be *set* to states that enable the execution this specific test case (instead of 'ending up' in a specific state via long set ups). For example, it is far more efficient to set a course to be full (via the relevant instance variable) than to create a number of students corresponding to this course's maximum size and then to add each of these students to the course!

Consequently, we adopt a representation of a test case that requires the VF to invoke the binding tool when required. Consider, for example for **TC1**, the following:

{ Create(context), Create(u), fire(CoursesCreated), Set(context,IsCreated(), true),
Set(context,IsFullTime(), false), Set(course,IsFull(), true),
Set(course,IsFull(), false), Set(course,IsFull(), false) }

The *Create* operation requires that the VF instantiate the required sole argument and then open the binding tool on it in order for the user to set all relevant instance variables. Events can be directly fired (i.e., no need to go through university in our example to fire *CoursesCreated*) in order to force a particular path of execution. Finally, the *Set* operation opens a binding tool on its first argument which must be an existing instance. The user then sets one or more variables of that instance. Then the second argument is called and its return value is compared to the third argument. The binding tool does not close before these two values match, ensuring that the selected branching is indeed executed.

In summary, in our VF, test case execution is semi-automatic: it requires that, during execution the binding tool be used to set some of the variables of the relevant instances in order to execute the selected path(s) through a scenario. It is left to the user to know which variables to set (e.g., student number must not be zero for *IsCreated* to return true). More sophisticated, less cumbersome approaches to test case generation would require that the VF carry out a deeper analysis of a scenario and of the responsibilities it refers to in order to determine which specific variables of which specific instances determine this scenario's flow of control. Such an analysis is currently beyond the scope of our work.

Finally, we emphasize that a fully automated purely static approach to test case generation and execution appears to be very difficult to achieve even using parameters. For example, the number of courses does vary from one test case to another for scenario ***RegisterForCourses***...

5 Conclusion

In this paper, we presented a tool that supports the *automated* validation of the requirements of the contractor against the *actual behavior* of an IUT delivered by the contracted. This is achieved via the automatic generation of executable test cases from a testable IUT-independent model of the requirements. A fair amount of experimentation and testing has been carried out on the VF. First, a comprehensive suite was used for the ACL compiler. Then, five extensive case studies [16] were developed to verify the handling of static and dynamic checks, as well as scenario monitoring and metrics evaluation. Finally, the tool was used in a graduate course one of the authors. The feedback we received stated clearly that, as with Spec#, ACL 'feels like' a programming language and thus may be of limited interest to the contractor and the testers alike. While we believe ACL's semantic richness is required to deal with industrial (i.e., non-toy) examples, the question is: what can be done? At this point in time, we believe the answer lies in understanding Meyer's seminal idea of programs that test themselves: the more errors will be automatically detectable within an IUT through the use of a programming language and tools such as AutoTest [15], the more the semantics of ACL and, in turn, requirements models captured using ACL will be simplified. Most importantly, such simplifications should also ultimately lead to a simpler if not more automated creation of bindings and of executable test cases.

Acknowledgments. Support from the Natural Science and Engineering Research Council of Canada is gratefully acknowledged.

References

1. Meyer, B.: The Unspoken Revolution in Software Engineering. IEEE Computer 39(1), 121–123 (2006)
2. Corriveau, J.-P.: Testable Requirements for Offshore Outsourcing. In: Meyer, B., Joseph, M. (eds.) SEAFOOD 2007. LNCS, vol. 4716, pp. 27–43. Springer, Heidelberg (2007)
3. Binder, R.: Testing Object-Oriented Systems. Addison-Wesley Professional, Reading (2000)
4. Grieskamp, W.: Multi-Paradigmatic Model-Based Testing. Technical Report #MSR-TR-2006-111, Microsoft Research (2006)
5. International Telecommunications Union: The Evolution of TTCN, `http://www.itu.int/ITU-T/studygroups/com17/ttcn.html`
6. Ryser, J., Glinz, M.: SCENT: A Method Employing Scenarios to Systematically Derive Test Cases for System Test. Technical Report. University of Zurich (2003)
7. Beck, K.: Test-Driven Development: By Example. Addison-Wesley, Reading (2002)
8. Arnold, D., Corriveau, J.-P., Shi, W.: Validation against Actual Behavior: Still a Challenge for Testing Tools. In: Software Engineering Research and Practice (SERP). CSREA Press (July 2010)
9. Cucumber, `http://cukes.info/`
10. Microsoft Research: Spec# Tool, `http://research.microsoft.com/specsharp`
11. Veanes, M., Campbell, C., Grieskamp, W., Nachmanson, L., Schulte, W., Tillmann, N.: Model-based testing of object-oriented reactive systems with Spec Explorer, Tech. Rep. MSR-TR-2005-59, Microsoft Research (2005)
12. Meyer, B.: Design by Contract. IEEE Computer 25(10), 40–51 (1992)
13. Arnold, D., Corriveau, J.-P., Shi, W.: Modeling and Validating Requirements using Executable Contracts and Scenarios. In: Software Engineering Research, Management & Applications (SERA 2010). Springer, Heidelberg (May 2010)
14. Buhr, R.J.A., Casselman, R.: Use Case Maps for Object Oriented Systems. Prentice Hall, New York (1995)
15. Meyer, B., Fiva, A., Ciupa, I., Leitner, A., Wei, Y., Stapf, E.: Programs that test themselves. IEEE Computer 42, 46–55 (2009)
16. Arnold, D., Corriveau, J.-P.: The Validation Framework and its examples, `http://vf.davearnold.ca/`
17. Briand, L., Labiche, Y.: A UML-Based Approach to System Testing. In: Gogolla, M., Kobryn, C. (eds.) UML 2001. LNCS, vol. 2185, pp. 194–208. Springer, Heidelberg (2001)
18. Nebut, C., Fleury, F., Le Traon, Y., Jézéquel, J.M.: Automatic Test Generation: A Use Case Driven Approach. IEEE Transactions on Software Engineering 32, 140–155 (2006)

Argentina's Offshore Software Industry – Opportunities and Challenges

Santiago Ceria[1] and Carlos Pallotti[2]

[1] University of Buenos Aires and Hexacta – Arguibel 2860, Buenos Aires (1426), Argentina
sceria@gmail.com
[2] Lupa Corporation – 25 de Mayo 583, Buenos Aires (1002), Argentina
carlos@lupacorp.com

Abstract. Argentina's software industry is orders of magnitude smaller than the largest software industries in the world like India's. However, it has seen impressive growth over the last years, with ratios ranging from 15 to 20% per year since 2003. This is due to several reasons, including time zone compatibility with the US and Europe, resource quality, price competitiveness and active policies from the local governments over the last 8 years. In particular, time zone compatibility has proved to be a significant advantage when using agile methodologies, as frequent interaction between stakeholders and the development teams is needed. In this paper we discuss in detail some of the reasons we believe have made this growth possible, along with some insights on the software engineering processes being used by some of the companies that have positioned themselves successfully in the offshore market. We finish by describing the strategy that is being followed by the government and IT chambers of commerce and associations to make this growth sustainable.

Keywords: Argentina offshore industry, distributed agile methods.

1 Introduction

Argentina's information technology industry has seen impressive growth since the economic crisis that the country suffered in the 2001-2002 period. In particular, the software development industry has shown a growth ratio ranging from 15% to 20% per year, beating the performance of the overall economy and creating a demand for local resources that could barely be satisfied by local universities and institutions. There are many reasons why this growth has been possible: price competitiveness, the quality of local resources and the good level of local universities, time zone compatibility, good language skills in the IT professionals and active policies from the last governments are some of them.

In this paper we describe some of those reasons and we present the challenges that this industry is facing. We also present some of the software engineering practices being applied by local companies that played a role in this success.

M. Nordio et al. (Eds.): SEAFOOD 2010, LNBIP 54, pp. 23–36, 2010.

1.1 The Argentine Software Sector at a Glance

Before the 2001-2002 economic crisis, Argentina's software sector was small and mainly focused on providing services to financial institutions and companies that had been privatized by the government during the 90's. The total number of people employed by the sector was around 15.000, and the amount of exports was negligible. In addition, it's worth mentioning that Argentina has one of the highest levels of education in the region. This has historically generated that many Argentine professionals and scientists decide to look for opportunities abroad.

Before the crisis generated an impact in the country's economy, the end of the process of privatization of public companies and the end of the effect of the Y2K caused that many companies started to explore external markets, opening commercial and services offices. When the crisis hit Argentina, the IT sector suffered a great impact in local revenues, as companies cancelled all their investment budgets, and thousands of IT professionals that were outsourced in those companies were returned to their providers. But, at the same time, due to the devaluation of the local currency by more than 200%, suddenly Argentina's costs became very competitive when measured in US dollars. Both factors pushed many companies to start exporting services, joining the few that had managed to gain external markets with an overvalued currency. Also, several start-ups were created to take advantage of the new competitive landscape.

In this new scenario, organizations of the IT sector and the government started to create a 10 year plan (2004-2014), to allow those competitive advantages to become sustainable in time, and to give this industry a window of opportunity for its growth. This plan was formalized in the "Blue and White Book" [1] and, together with additional promotional actions, attracted some international companies to open software development centers in the country. Examples are Motorola, who was the pioneer is 2001, IBM, Intel, Sabre, Oracle, Accenture, CapGemini and SAP.

As a consequence of what is described above, in 2009 Argentina's software industry reached 60.000 employed professionals. The following chart shows some important data about the progression of key indicators:

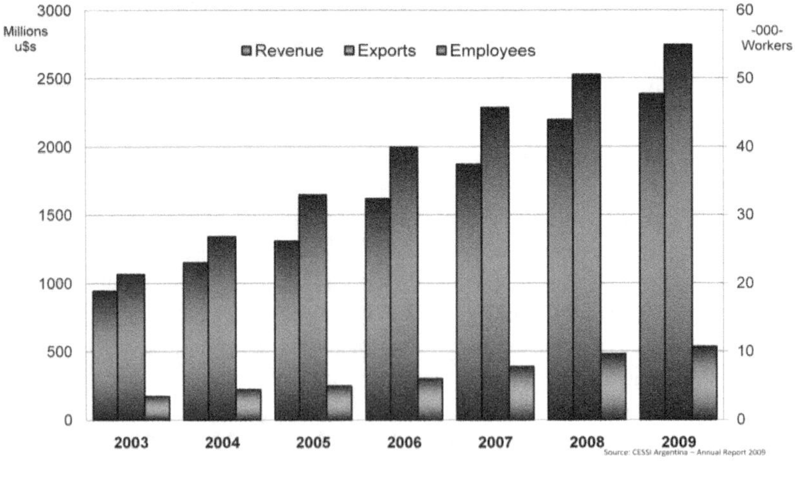

Fig. 1. Argentina's software industry's key indicators

Even with all these positive news and data, there's consensus in government officials and chambers of commerce and associations that the size of our software industry requires a strategy that is not based on price competitiveness and on high volumes but one based on high value added. We describe the strategy being followed in section 4.

1.2 Organization of the Paper

In section 2 we present our view on some of the reasons for Argentina's offshore industry's success. In section 3 we discuss some software engineering techniques and practices being used by some of the country's successful companies. In section 4 we present the ValueShore – ValueSoft model that sets a target for where our industry is heading. We conclude in section 5 with some final thoughts about this experience and the future of our industry.

2 Some Reasons for Argentina's Offshore Industry's Success

In this section we discuss some of the reasons we believe have made this growth possible. Of course part of this is due to external forces, including growth in the demand for these services. However, we believe that many of them are due to good decisions that were made locally and other local historical and social factors.

2.1 Price/Quality Competitiveness

There's an important consensus in the local industry that a good relation between price and quality is a strong fundamental for an industry to be based on. As in most non central countries, in Argentina the macroeconomic variables tend to have significant fluctuations, including an over or sub valuation of the currency. In this context, we think that it is crucial to preserve the competitive conditions while keeping a convenient relationship between a reasonable price and the best possible quality in the services provided. Basing an industry only in low prices could mean that variations in macroeconomic conditions affect the possibility of reaching or maintaining markets.

Nowadays, many years after the local plan started to be applied, Argentina maintains reasonably low prices, though higher than the ones from the immediate years after the devaluation and also higher than those of other offshore providers. For example, a yearly salary for a senior developer ranges from USD 21,000 to 24,000 in Argentina, while in India the average is close to USD 13,000. However, as companies have strived to increase the quality levels of the services provided by training the workforce and by pursuing quality certifications, the relationship between price and quality has remained constant, allowing the industry not to lose competitiveness. Just to mention an example related to quality, Argentina ranks number 12 in the countries with most CMMI SCAMPI-A evaluations, with a total of 69, while India ranks number 3 with 460 and Mexico number 13 with 68[2].

2.2 Active Policies from Local Government

Argentina's last three governments (2002-2010) have worked actively in promoting the software industry, following the plan mentioned above. A few examples are described:

- In 2004, the law 25.922 –called the "software law" – was passed. This law provides tax incentives, tax stability and other benefits to software development companies as long as they export software services, pursue quality certifications (CMMI or ISO) and dedicate significant resources to R&D. More than 450 companies are now receiving those benefits.
- The government has also promoted high level education, offering incentives to young students to pursue IT related careers.
- Through a program carried out together by the Ministry of Education and local companies, more than 30.000 people have been trained in current technologies.
- The current administration has promoted Science and Technology to a Ministry and provided it with more specific funds for the development of basic and applied science.
- In addition, and by the action of this new Ministry, the government has created the Manuel Sadosky Foundation [3], which will be a network of R&D centers with participation of the two main IT chambers of commerce.
- The government is working on a digital plan, through a "digital agenda", prepared in collaboration with the private sector, so that we can have in the 2010-2016 period a better use of information technology, not only for the administration itself, but also to provide the benefits of the digital era to a larger population.
- The state, the private sector and the education system have coincided in a plan, which has been applied for the last four years, which is targeted to transform Argentina in year 2014 in a leader between non central countries in some specific areas related to information technology [4].
- Following the example of the 2004-2014 plan, a prospective study focused on how to achieve successful IT sector in 2020 was conducted under coordination of the Ministry of Science and Technology [5].

2.3 Quality of Local Resources

Although political instability during the second part of last century also affected it, Argentina still takes pride on its education system, which is public and free, and on its scientific system, which made it the only country in the region to have 3 Nobel Prize winners in sciences. Argentina had some computer pioneers during the 60's, such as Manuel Sadosky, who promoted the import of the first computer for scientific purposes, Clementina, in 1960.

The following chart shows data about tertiary enrollment published by the World Bank:

Reports from the Ministry of Education show that, in 2007, 85,497 students were following computing related university careers. There were 236 active careers in 52 Universities, with 80% of the students studying in public universities and the rest in private ones. Careers vary in content and length, the shorter ones lasting 4 years and the longer ones a minimum of 5 to 6 years. All of them have the requisite of a complete secondary education, implying a total of 14 years of education before getting to the University. During 2007, the government implemented a tertiary studies program with duration of two to three years. This generated 104 new careers and a total of 9,200 new enrollees.

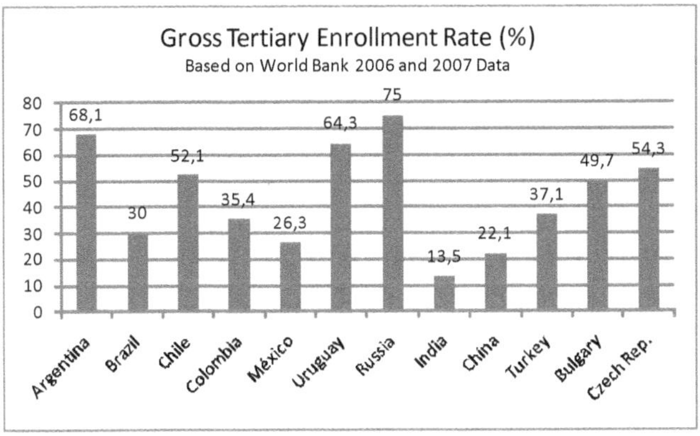

Fig. 2. Tertiary enrollment (%) based on World Bank data

2.4 Muticultural Environment

Many Argentines that live in the country's largest cities are descendants from immigrants that came to Argentina in the late 19th century until past the 2nd World War. This created a multiethnic population with more ease for speaking other languages. Also, there's a long tradition of teaching English in Argentine schools. It's now mandatory in primary schools in several regions of the country, including the city of Buenos Aires. This plays a critical role in the offshore industry.

This multiethnic environment also probably plays a role in the cultural affinity that can be seen between Argentine professionals and clients from US and European countries. Argentina's professionals are creative and tend to propose new ideas and to challenge existing ones when projects are being executed. Although difficult to quantify, these factors seem to be making a contribution to the success of our industry, and are frequently mentioned by foreign managers hiring Argentina teams.

Argentina also has a strong entrepreneur culture. According to a study of the Global Entrepreneurship Monitor, Argentina had position number 16th in the ranking of entrepreneur countries in 2006 [6]. Also in that year, more than 10% of companies were new or recent, a similar level to what can be found in countries with strong entrepreneurship culture such as the US or Canada.

3 Software Engineering Techniques

In this section we provide some examples of software engineering approaches used by local companies. It's based mainly on the experience of Hexacta, the company where one of the authors works, but has been enriched with input from software engineering specialists from other companies that have successfully exported software to very demanding destinations such as the US and Europe. The Hexacta experience is mainly on developing custom software using Java and .Net technologies. The company has now around 200 professionals, and the typical project requires between 5 to 10 full time employees. About 70% or the company's revenues come from exports to the US and Europe. The readers should take into account that Aregntina's Software Industry is much broader, and the following sections are only presented as examples.

3.1 Challenges of Offshore Development

Remote software development has always presented challenges, as this activity requires frequent interaction between team members and interaction is naturally complicated by distance. With the methodologies used in the past decades, where developers and managers relied heavily in documentation for communication, the problem was partially solved if adequate processes were used. However, as agile methods started to gain momentum in software development, a new challenge was presented. The debate on whether it's possible to do agile development from distant locations while respecting all the principles of agile manifesto is still open and probably will be for many years. However, we can present successful cases of using agile methods with offshore teams, which can be added to several papers and experience reports describing similar successes that have been published in several conferences [7], [8]. There are many techniques that have proved to be critical for this success. In the following points we describe some of them:

1. Choosing the right methods – the role of agile methods
2. Choosing the right team configuration
3. Using adequate tools
4. Improving daily interaction

3.2 Choosing the Right Methods – The Role of Agile Methods

Agile methods have an increasing presence in the software engineering landscape. They are a collection of effective software engineering practices – some new, some old – that provide excellent results. However, many of the outsourced projects require turnkey estimations and commitments, and this presents a challenge when methods that welcome change are used. In the case of Hexacta, two different methodology approaches are used when performing offshore projects:

- When a fixed estimation is required, a method with more focus on requirements change control is used. The iterative and incremental lifecycle model is used, but a Change Control Board exists in order to evaluate change requests and assess their impact on the project. In this type of projects, the notion of "Phases" to which iterations belong, such as in the Rational Unified Process®, is very helpful.
- When a team is contracted using a flexible approach, agile methods are used with the combination of Scrum for organizing the team and the work and some Extreme Programming practices for improving productivity and quality.

Although experts in different methods prefer to keep them pure and discourage the combination of practices or their partial use, we have seen in different projects that it is possible for example to incorporate agile practices such as continuous integration to projects using a more traditional methodology.

In the following sections we will refer to cases where the agile methodology is used, taking into account that it generates more interest in industry.

3.3 Choosing the Right Team Configuration

A Scrum team is composed by three roles: a Scrum Master, a Product Owner, and The Team. The typical configuration for offshore projects that we have seen work is to have a team together with its Scrum Master, while the Product Owner is remote. The following points provide some insight on some of the things we've seen work when setting up team configurations:

- In many cases it's good to have a "proxy" to the Product Owner working together with the team. Ideally this person would be a functional expert in the business. This facilitates communication between team members and the Product Owner. The proxy can be any team member.
- It is possible to have a part of the team working locally and a part working remotely. For example, two offshore developers working together with two developers from the client working at the client's site. This pushes further the problem of communication, but we think it can be done as long as the developers share the same repositories and can meet daily in a daily standup using a videoconferencing system. In this sense, time zone compatibility is more than great help, it becomes necessary.
- Scrum Masters have to be where the team is, to provide their leadership. However, Scrum Masters also have to be where the impediments are, to resolve them. Sometimes impediments are at the client's site, and therefore the Scrum Master needs some representative there to help with these impediments.

3.4 Using Adequate Tools

Tools play a key role in successful offshore teams. The following are the most important ones according to our experience:

- A tool for managing the backlog and work in progress will be needed as the effectiveness of a taskboard is limited when the team is distributed. We have used several tools for this purpose with excellent results.
- Repositories have to be shared. Different teams need to check in code to the same repositories. The continuous integration tools have to affect all teams.
- A videoconferencing system has to be used for daily standups.

3.5 Improving Daily Interaction

One of the keys of agile methods is face to face communication. For evident reasons, this is not possible with remote teams. In our case, we've mitigated the negative impact of this by interacting frequently during the day with chats and emails, and also by briefly extending daily standups to allow for communication between the team and the product owner to discuss backlog related issues. So in our case the script of daily standups deviates slightly from the standard.

4 The ValueShore – ValueSoft Model

4.1 The Need for the Model

Growth has to be sustainable to constitute real economic possibilities for the country. In order to make it sustainable, it is necessary to discuss fundamental topics, in particular those that are the basis for models which might be followed. There are many examples of countries of delayed entry that penetrated high-tech markets, especially in the industry of software development or provision of information services of various complexities. Some of them have become very successful while others have not. Nevertheless, they allow contemplating various public policies or private activities which have given different results.

Not all successful models can be repeated and it is also impossible to avoid repeating certain mistakes in other contexts. However, the companies that are well intellectually prepared have the capacity to analyze such phenomena, to take account of specific conditions of their environment and consider future scenarios and then create their own plans based on such experience.

In a SWOT analysis prepared by Argentina's software companies chamber of commerce (CESSI) included in [3] there are several items that support the need to elaborate concepts of the ValueShore-ValueSoft (VS) model. For example, most of the strengths arise from the existence of a level of education still interesting for the emerging countries and the concern in the search for associability. We can also emphasize that the fact that Argentina may be seen as a qualified producer, i.e. with certain distinctive aspects compared to its potential competitors, is presented as an opportunity. But it is a serious weakness that the country has not yet implemented the Argentinean mark which would identify us as a "technological" country, as well as the limited possibility for growth of the number of human resources qualified to be employed in our sector. This is even more obvious when we analyze the threats because of the existence of tension between the demand for growth and the education of human resources that would enable it.

To summarize, if Argentina wants to concentrate on a growth project, then it must do so bearing in mind its capacity to generate high-quality human resources but limited in number. This means, it has to focus on the quality of growth (measured as higher productivity of its workforce) rather than just quantity.

4.2 Description of the Model

As many experiences show, the worldwide situation permits to be optimistic about the possibility of growth for our industry. But this growth has to be adjusted to what our country is able to do, both due to its cultural environment and its economic structure and to the maturity of its industry. As we mentioned in the introduction, Argentina has clear advantages compared to other countries in the region, especially when weighing values related to education and human resources. However, our competitors are not countries in the region but the rest of the world and this is why it is necessary to analyze the topic from a global point of view.

There are three clear examples in the world of leadership by the countries of late entry to the IT market: India, Ireland and Israel, although there are other cases that could also arise from the comparative analysis. We know that in Argentina, the software industry has an existing workforce of approximately 60,000 persons working in about 1000 companies, the forecast being to have 65,000 to 70,000 by the end of 2011.

If we remember that countries such as India have a production capacity of qualified human resources at least thirty times higher than Argentina's and that the demand of worldwide markets requires volumes that Argentina can never think of supplying considering the Argentinean population (41 million), we can infer that it is not the volume where growth may be achieved. Actually, nowadays less than 0.3% of the economically active population works in the software industry and slightly more than 2% in the whole technology-based industry, including activities such as communications and call centers. Furthermore, less than 5% of university students study related careers. Therefore, one may expect growth in the number of trained people but restricted by the limits referred to above.

Some other factors that add to the above are not less important when it comes to a deeper analysis. First, our country is not, at the international macroeconomic level, cheap. Our professionals and technicians have the same level of requirements concerning the quality of life as their European or American peers. The exchange rate differences or factors not related to the sector can make the offer temporarily competitive, but these conditions cannot be sustained permanently. For example, until 2001 we were one of the most expensive countries for software development (however, and partially this is one of the arguments that we hold, companies such as Motorola Corporation decided to locate a development center at that time).

Also, the average profile of a professional or technician in Argentina corresponds to the criteria of being innovative and creative much more than systemic (i.e. to follow pre-established instructions to produce something). This is possibly due to the influence of European immigration to our country or other cultural reasons but it is certain that we do not like very much to use pre-established procedures or fixed rules for the development of products or processes. On the contrary, we show creativity when it comes to facing challenges and this is reflected in the fact that designers, architects or programmers tend to offer or include new and better features into the products when they are presented with a specification. Therefore, it would be against the cultural nature of the average profile of our people to try to focus on a model based on a business of mass consumption of systemic resources when they present a better facet in a creative environment.

However, to analyze these possibilities it is necessary to understand the value chain in the SIS industry.

The chart above illustrates the form of this chain and how each part works in the generation of value. On the left side there are activities (or companies) that invest heavily in research and development and, naturally, add a lot of value to the economy. In the worldwide context, we will notice there companies such as Microsoft, Google, Intel, IBM and many others. For illustration only, the chart includes estimated values in Argentinean pesos of what would be the annual productivity of the workforce there in worldwide terms (measured as total annual income vs. the total number of persons to achieve such income).

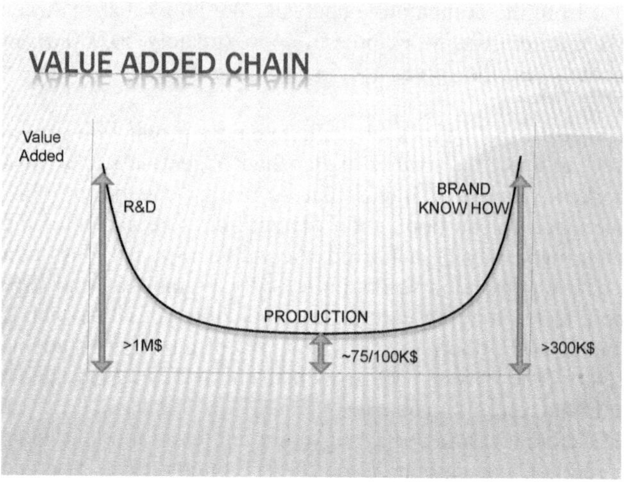

Fig. 3. The Value Added Chain

As we are moving to the right, we will find sectors where the added value is lower. These are sectors related to different activities, such as development of applications derived from other technologies, production of custom-made software, coding, testing, customer care services, etc., to name just a few. These are sectors where the demand is higher in terms of use of human resources.

Finally, there is growth of value at the moment of creating specific brands or abilities that allow obtaining a differential in the offer. They are shown on the right side of the chart. This explains why a client purchases services from a specific company and not a similar one although the first might result more expensive. This is due to the simple fact that the client understands that such a company has better knowledge of the issue in question or a reputation in the market that makes it more reliable.

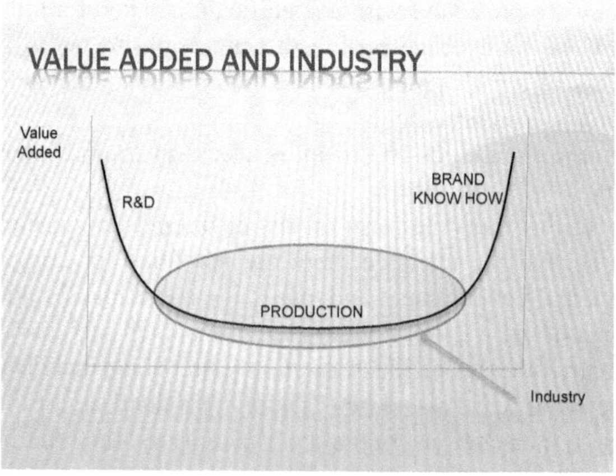

Fig. 4. Argentina's Current Situation in the Value Chain

The same chart shows approximately where we can currently find the Argentinean industry. We have companies that develop applications with higher or lower degree of complexity and R&D content without reaching the products of the highest scale that would be placed on the left side of the chart. There are also companies that provide information services with added value whether due to having created a corporate brand or due to being familiar with the "rules of business" of certain specific niches that allow them to differentiate their offer from that of their competitors.

Nevertheless, there is a major core concentrated in the average zone of production, represented by companies that provide services where a great part of their income is based on provision of man-hours of various types. Many of these companies have shown to be good at managing this type of business but they have worldwide competence and the prices are mostly commoditized.

4.3 The Projected Industry

India is well known for its capacity to be a major provider of offshore services, concerning not only software development but also other related services, such as BPO, calls centers, etc. The eastern European countries are trying to get a share in this market as well as many other regions, including other Latin American countries.

Blanca Treviño, president of SOFTEK, a successful Mexican company, patented the name *Near Shore* as a way to be different from the offer of other countries, saying "I can do the same but nearer, in the same time zone and within no more than four hours by plane".

As previously seen, Argentina is not able to openly compete in offshore with any chance of being a relevant player, nor can it say that it is close to the central markets, at least geographically. However, it can show its qualities renowned worldwide at the educational and cultural levels, and it can present itself as a provider of offshore with more value added. We will name this strategy ValueShore.

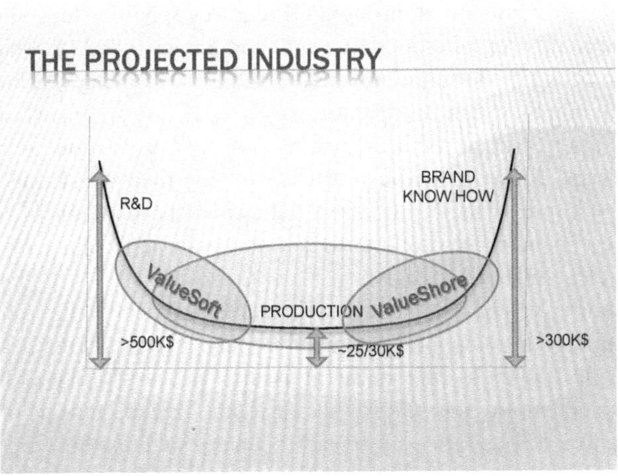

Fig. 5. Argentina's Projected Industry

But what kinds of services are offered within this concept? It is a wide scope ranging from provision of services with contents (for example, e-learning), development of interactive applications using dynamic web technologies (for example, advert-games), specific applications that require the use of innovative technologies and implementation of integral projects where the cost of labor would not be the essential element but would remain covered by other advantages, to provision of services in specific economic environments or sectors where the knowledge of the companies differentiates the offer from the rest. This is a very brief summary given the many areas of application. We should call this ValueShore and Argentina would have every right to claim for itself the motto "A great place for Valueshore". This is like saying "if you need high-quality services with distinctive features, approach our companies".

Along the same line, we may analyze what is happening at the other end with ValueSoft. This word may not be as illustrative as the previous one and it could cause some confusion. Actually, many countries might argue that they are suitable to make "ValueSoft". But what we are trying to explain through this concept is that Argentina can be good at developing specialized products in particular technological or economic sectors, i.e. customized products for specific markets and sophisticated in a way.

Argentina should propose this concept of VS which should be considered at the moment of analyzing the type of investments and/or promotion of entrepreneurialism. As we can see, the way to achieve the objectives is not to encourage establishment of the companies by cheap workforce. On the contrary, it could only put off the possibility to create a healthy and, above all, sustainable local industry. That is why it should be interesting to propose investments that use our country for the development of services or applications focused on added value. On the contrary, creating the "intensive workforce" market without adding value would only make the activity rise but it would be difficult for it to develop in the mid-term.

Naturally, the growth gained through VS requires specific steps allowing the companies to move in this sense, especially small companies that do not have the financial or managerial back-up. That would enable them to implement changes in quality while they maintain their current operations.

The ValueShore concept requires, among other things, actions related to facilitating access to loans allowing the businesses to extend their operations, expand abroad or significantly improve their processes. Likewise, the creation of a country brand will help the companies get support from it and gain better chances of offering services, such as those referred to above.

The ValueSoft concept also requires financing, especially for R&D activities, in addition to support for companies that need to change the existing activities for those that might be desirable. In this sense, it is also necessary that existing (or to-be-created) R&D centers are able to provide basic intelligence for our products. Entities such as the Sadosky Foundation or research centers such as those planned in various provinces would be, without doubts, necessary steps in this sense.

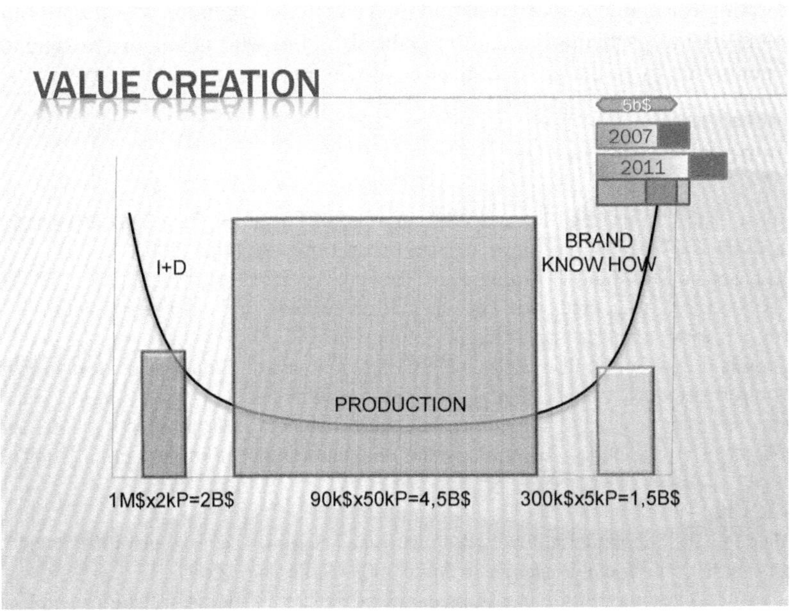

Fig. 6. Potential Benefits of the Model

5 Conclusions

Let us conclude with some words on expectable results.

On the above chart, we want to show what could be, in a rough outline, the values of income that could be earned in every case.

We are aware that not the entire sector can move towards the VS models as mentioned above but if at least a part of them does, it will result in a net increase of the annual revenue of at least 3,500 million pesos. This could eventually mean a growth higher than 75% of what may naturally be reached to date, with the additional note that the required specialized human resources would be limited to no more than 7,000 people working in these key sectors. To summarize, this means to take advantage of the benefits of the boom with a mass model (in line with the actual possibilities of the country), but adding an important quota, benefit of higher productivity in key areas related to ValueShore and ValueSoft, as we have seen.

To achieve this, a series of steps should be taken that would help to maintain this selected intellectual capital, increasing also its level of education and training. But at the same time we have to encourage companies to make this important change.

To conclude, we would like to make it very clear that this study on VS does not pretend to conclude that it is the only possible way of growth for Argentina or that the remaining areas not mentioned here should not be taken into account.

Acknowledgments. The list of people that have contributed indirectly to this paper is too large to be included, as several people from industry and academia have been collaborating for many years to promote the growth of Argentina's Software Industry. We would like to particularly mention Gabriel Baum, who is one of the fundamental forces behind many of the good things that are being done in our Country in this front.

References

1. Software and IT Services Blue and White Book. SITS Strategic Plan 2004-2014 and Action Plan 2004-2007. Ministry of Economy and Production, Argentina (2004)
2. Data based on SEI Maturity Profile, `http://www.sei.cmu.edu/cmmi/casestudies/profiles/`
3. `http://www.fundacionsadosky.com.ar`
4. Proposals for an Action Plan 2008-2011, CESSI, Cámara de Empresas de Software y Servicios Informáticos (September 2009), `http://www.cessi.org.ar`
5. Baum, G., Artopoulos, A. (coordinators).: Libro Blanco de la prospectiva TIC, Proyecto 2020. Ministry of Science, Technology and Production Innovation, Argentina (2009)
6. `http://www.clarin.com/diario/2007/03/29/conexiones/t-01389418.htm`
7. Sutherland, J., Schoonheim, G.: Fully Distributed Scrum: Linear Scalability of Production Between SFO and India. Presented at Agile 2009 Conference (2009)
8. Miller, A.: Distributed Agile Development. Experiences at Microsoft Patterns and Practices. Presented at Agile 2009 Conference (2009)

Model-Based Task Allocation in Distributed Software Development

Ansgar Lamersdorf[1] and Jürgen Münch[1,2]

[1] University of Kaiserslautern
[2] Fraunhofer IESE
a_lamers@informatik.uni-kl.de,
Juergen.Muench@iese.fraunhofer.de

Abstract. Task allocation is one central aspect in planning and managing global software development projects. To date several models that support task allocation have been proposed, including cost models and risk-based approaches. However, systematic integration of such models and a guiding process for task allocation activities is widely missing. In this article, we integrate existing models that reflect different viewpoints and abstraction levels of task allocation decisions. Based on the integrated approach, we sketch a process for systematic evaluation and selection of task assignments that defines the model interfaces and the sequential order of their use. In detail, the approach presented here integrates a risk model that is able to identify the possible risks for each assignment individually, an optimization model that uses Bayesian networks to suggest assignment alternatives with respect to multiple criteria, and an effort overhead model that is able to estimate the project effort for each assignment alternative. All three models are significantly grounded in empirical studies. Besides the introduction of all three models and the description of the process, the article provides an example application, sketches related work, and presents an overview of future work.

1 Introduction

Every software development project – be it in offshoring or outsourcing – that involves work from different, distributed sites requires a decision about task allocation: How can the individual tasks that together constitute the development project be distributed across the available sites?

There are many different ways to allocate tasks to different sites, especially with respect to the division of work into different tasks and with respect to criteria for deciding where tasks will be enacted: The work can be divided by process steps, along architectural components, by functionality, or using combinations of these models [1] [2]. In an extensive empirical study on the practice of distributed development, we identified three main criteria for task allocation: labor cost rates, availability of people, and expertise [3]. The cost rate, in particular, is often reported as a major criterion for task allocation: In global development, work is mainly assigned to those sites that have the lowest labor cost rates [4] [5].

M. Nordio et al. (Eds.): SEAFOOD 2010, LNBIP 54, pp. 37–53, 2010.

However, despite the differences, we observed that, in general, the assignment of work is done rather unsystematically in practice, without any specific process or defined decision procedure [3]. The criteria for work allocation are not defined systematically and are often just applied by the responsible project manager based on personal experiences. This highly increases the risks of distributed development projects, as there are many problems in global software development that are influenced by the task allocation decision: Language, cultural, and time zone differences are just some examples of barriers between sites that may cause problems such as decreased productivity [6] and increased lack of trust [7]. Assigning work to sites with low differences reduces these barriers and the resulting problems (often referred to as "nearshoring" [8]). Other problems such as high turnover rates [9] and little knowledge of the customer or application domain are also influenced by assigning work to different sites. Together with the already mentioned criteria for work allocation (labor cost rates, availability, expertise) this shows that the task allocation decision is highly complex and should take into account multiple criteria and influencing factors in order to reduce or avoid the problems immanent in distributed and global software development (GSD).

There are different perspectives under which a task allocation decision could be regarded: From a risk management perspective, there are various risks specific to GSD that are influenced by the work assignment (e.g., assigning work to sites with large cultural differences increases the risk of mistrust between sites). Thus, any given task allocation alternative can be evaluated under the perspective of the potential risks it creates. From the perspective of a project planner, one specific task allocation has to be selected from the (potentially large) pool of alternatives, taking into account multiple, sometimes conflicting, goals and influencing factors. Finally, the cost perspective requires special attention in GSD, as low labor costs are one driving factor for global development. However, since the distribution of work has an impact on both labor cost rates and productivity, any task allocation alternative should also be evaluated under the perspective of effort and cost estimation.

While all three perspectives are clearly different, they all regard the same decision and phenomena. Thus, they underlying influencing factors and causal relationships are common to all perspectives. In this article, we present an approach for systematic task allocation that includes models for all three of these perspectives and integrates them into one process for evaluating and selecting task allocation alternatives. The individual models have already been published separately [10], [11], [12], [13] but have not yet been integrated into one decision process as presented here.

The remainder of this article is structured as follows: Section 2 gives an overview of related work in task allocation decision support from different perspectives. Section 3 explains the task allocation process by briefly introducing the three sub-models and then presenting the process that integrates all models into one task allocation decision. Section 4 gives an example of how the process can be applied to an industrial context. Finally, Section 5 concludes the article and gives an overview of future work.

2 Related Work

Task allocation in global software development has been the focus of several research approaches and has already been analyzed in detail in another publication

[14]. We will thus just briefly highlight some related work in this area. There exist some research papers on the processes and criteria currently applied in practice that are based on empirical studies and observations [1] [15] [3]. However, they do not or only rudimentarily provide decision support for future GSD projects.

Few approaches have been developed in research that explicitly provide decision support in task allocation. Mockus and Weiss [2] developed an algorithm that identifies pieces of work (in this case, the responsibility for modules of the software) as candidates that should be reassigned from one site to another. The criterion for the assignment is minimization of cross-site communication as this highly influences distributed development overhead. Other criteria and influencing factors (e.g., cost rates, expertise, barriers between sites) were not regarded, however.

Setamanit et al. [16] [17] suggested a simulation model that is able to compare different task allocation strategies with respect to productivity and development time. It uses different influencing factors as input, such as familiarity, work coupling, and site-specific productivity. However, the model is rather designed for evaluating general strategies than for giving specific decision support for individual projects.

There are some other research approaches that aim at supporting task allocation in GSD projects, for example by developing an index for comparing coordination between sites [18], describing the work of a central coordination team [19], or defining a reference process for project planning in GSD [20]. However, none of them provides a comprehensive approach for task allocation in distributed projects.

From a risk management perspective, there exist different research approaches that try to assess risks specifically for distributed development projects. Ralyte et al. [21] developed a framework for potential risks in distributed and global software development. The risks are categorized along the two dimensions distance and activity. The framework only names possible risks and mitigation strategies; it does not say under which circumstances the risks might occur, nor does it describe the impact of task allocation on project risks.

Similarly, Ebert et al. [22] name risks and problems that are likely to occur in GSD projects together with mitigation strategies. This approach, too, does not name the impact of work allocation on risks.

Smite [23] developed a risk barometer that can help to identify project-specific risks. Thus, this approach is less generic and can be customized to individual projects. However, the described risks are again not impacted by task allocation.

In general, these risk management approaches show that the impact of task allocation on project risks has not yet been the focus of research. However, many risks described in the literature can be traced back to the barriers between sites and thus are clearly dependent on the decision about which sites work should be assigned to.

From an effort and cost estimation perspective, there also exist approaches that try to describe the cost overhead of distributed development. They are usually based on COCOMO2 [24], as this cost model is widely known and accepted.

One approach followed by different researchers [5] [25] is the extension of COCOMO2 using new cost drivers that specifically address distributed development. This includes drivers that are dependent on task allocation, such as cultural differences or the outsourcing maturity of the vendor. However, this does not take into account that many of the already existing cost drivers of COCOMO (e.g., programmer capability) might be different for every involved site and cannot be regarded globally (as it is done in COCOMO).

This problem is addressed by Madachy [26]. In this model, the original model of COCOMO is split up into several sub-models, which describe the characteristics of every involved site individually and which are then aggregated. Thus, the approach can support task allocation decisions by giving cost estimations that depend on the characteristics of the involved sites. However, it does not regard the overhead resulting from the barriers between sites and its impact on effort and costs.

In general, the existing cost estimation approaches do not regard all relevant aspects of distributed development, namely the different characteristics at the involved sites and the overhead due to distributed collaboration. Thus, they cannot be used to evaluate different task assignment alternatives with respect to the expected effort and costs. In addition, none of the analyzed approaches provides a sound empirical basis for the selection and quantification of the used cost drivers.

Looking at the related work from the three perspectives task allocation suggestion, risk identification in task allocation, and effort estimation, it can be seen that even though there exist several approaches in all of these areas that can support selected aspects of task allocation in GSD projects, there exists no comprehensive approach that can be used for systematic task allocation. This underlines the need for an approach that integrates all the different perspectives in order to provide decision support for task assignment.

3 Process Overview

In this section, the approach for task allocation decision support will be introduced. It consists of three different models, each regarding a specific perspective. Figure 1 gives an overview of the models together with the input needed for model development and the interfaces between them. In the following, we will present all three models individually, followed by a definition of the overall process for using the three models in task allocation decisions.

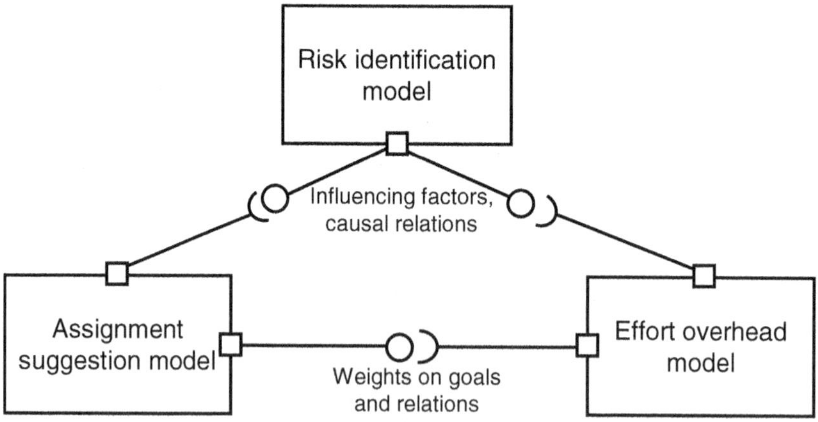

Fig. 1. Overview of models and relationships in model development

3.1 Risk Identification Model

The risk identification model is able to identify specific risks and problems of distributed development based on a characterization of the individual project and its involved sites. Using experiences from past projects as input, the model consists of logical rules describing potential threats and the influences that cause these risks.

Table 1 gives an example of how an experience (for example collected in interviews with experienced project managers) can be transferred into a rule describing the impact of an influencing factor on a project risk.

Table 1. Development of risk model based on collected experiences

Collected experience	*"If you have a distributed team then it needs to be informed every time. If you have one single team, the management needs to inform only one team. [...] the more sites, the more the number of teams that have to be coordinated"*
Influencing factors and risks	Influencing factors: • Number of sites Risks: • Coordination problems
Textual Rule	The more sites there are, the more people have to interact with each other in order to make any kind of decision and let the others know about it.
Logical Rule	Number of sites →+ Coordination problem

The considered project risks stem from the collected experiences but can be further specified and refined based on individual project goals and priorities.

As a result, the model consists of a set of influencing factors in distributed software development and logical rules that describe how these factors affect project risks (and thus, indirectly, project goals). The influencing factors are categorized into (1) characteristics of the project, (2) characteristics of the involved sites, (3) relationships between the involved sites, and (4) characteristics of the tasks assigned to the sites.

The model can be used twofold: On the one hand, it can be used for evaluating GSD projects and task assignment alternatives. Based on the characteristics of the involved sites (and therefore, indirectly, on the assignment decision), the rules predict different threats and problems that are likely to occur in a project and can help to compare different alternatives. On the other hand, the identified influencing factors and causal relationships are used as a basis for the subsequent models.

A prototype of a risk identification model has already been developed based on the analysis of 19 qualitative interviews with experienced practitioners in GSD. The created model was then evaluated at a Spanish software development company by comparing the predictions with the experiences from past projects. The result indicated that over 80 percent of the predicted risks had actually occurred in past projects. In addition, a group of five experienced managers all judged the model as very helpful for project management in future GSD projects.

3.2 Assignment Suggestion Model

The assignment suggestion model is able to identify assignment alternatives from the pool of all possibilities. This is done based on an internal Bayesian network model and the project characterization and goal weights done by the responsible project manager. It is described in detail in several other publications [14] [10] [11] [12]. Bayesian networks were chosen for different reasons: On the one hand, they are able to describe causal relations under uncertainty which, in our view, reflects the inherent nature of human behavior. On the other hand, they possess a graphical representation that makes it very easy for other persons (such as project managers) to understand the modeled concepts and causal relationships. Therefore, they have been used for software development project management in several occasions [27].

The model builds on a Bayesian network that describes influencing factors (again categorized into characteristics of tasks, sites, and the projects and relationships between sites), project goals (e.g., cost, time, quality), and causal relationships that model how the project goals are affected by the influencing factors. These relationships are weighted according to their relative impact. As Bayesian networks describe statistical relationships between factors, the relationships are able to cover the uncertainty in modeling human behavior. Figure 2 gives an excerpt of a Bayesian network used in the model. The network consists of variables (influencing factors or project goals), depicted as ovals, and causal relationships between them.

Using this Bayesian network, the model is able to assess the outcome of an assignment alternative with respect to weighted project goals. We implemented an algorithm that is able to automatically evaluate all possible assignments of tasks to sites for a given project and, as a result, rank them according to their expected fulfillment of the weighted goals [10]. This result thus represents a ranked list of assignment suggestions with respect to individual project characteristics and goals.

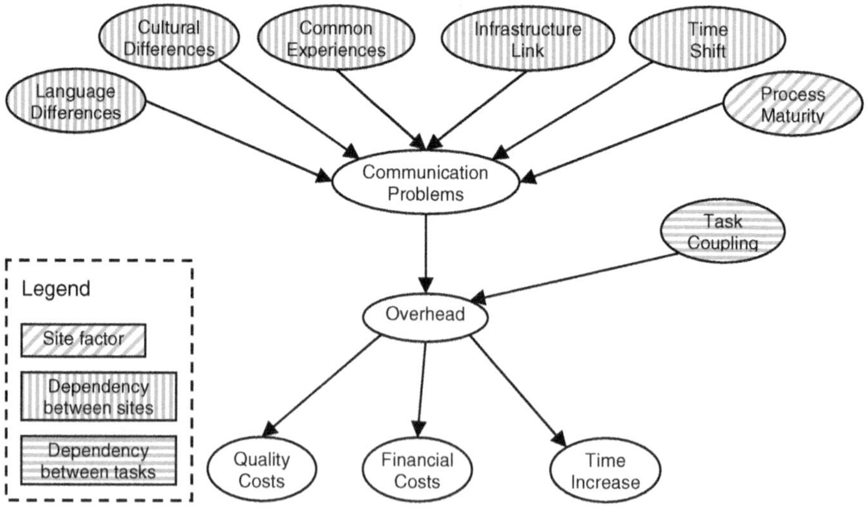

Fig. 2. Excerpt from Bayesian network model [10]

The underlying Bayesian network model can be easily modified and adapted to individual organizational contexts. For this, the results of the risk identification model can be used as input: In the risk identification model, influencing factors and causal relationships have already been defined. Thus, it remains for the Bayesian network to define how the identified risks affect project goals and to weigh the causal relationships against each other. This should again be done based on the estimations of experienced practitioners.

We developed a first prototype of the assignment suggestion. The underlying Bayesian network was developed based on an intensive literature study [12] and refined in interviews with nine highly experienced practitioners [10]. As a result, we implemented it as a Java tool, which has been presented in different publications [10] [11].

3.3 Effort Overhead Model

The effort overhead model is able to predict project effort based on a specific assignment decision and can thus be used to compare and evaluate assignment alternatives with respect to the expected project costs. It relies on the assumption that most software development organizations are able to estimate the effort for collocated projects effectively (e.g., using standard cost models like COCOMO or expert estimations), but experience unexpected overhead in distributed development projects. Consequently, the model aims at assessing the effort overhead that occurs in GSD projects.

We assume that the effort overhead in GSD is caused by two main phenomena that were already considered in existing effort models for GSD: First, there are different abilities (e.g., with respect to programmers' skills) at the involved sites [26]. This can be described using characteristics of the sites and the tasks assigned to these sites. Second, there are additional overhead drivers that are caused by the distances between sites [5] and that mainly depend on the relationships between sites. The effort overhead is thus influenced by the same factors and causal relationships as the overhead already identified in the other models.

For evaluating the effort overhead, the influencing factors and effort drivers have to be quantified. For this, we selected the CoBRA process [28] [29], which describes how a cost model can be developed based on a causal model and systematic expert quantifications. In a different publication [13], we show how the effort model can be used to assess and compare different assignment alternatives. By multiplying the predicted effort per site with the site-specific labor cost rates, the model is also used for evaluating task assignments with respect to overall project costs.

The influencing factors and causal relationships can be reused from the risk identification model (however, only those factors and relationships that influence productivity should be considered here). In addition, the weights identified in the assignment suggestion model can be used as a starting point for quantifying the impact. Thus, the effort overhead model should be developed last.

We also developed a prototype for the effort overhead model using expert estimations at a Spanish software development company. With an initial set of influencing factors taken from risk model development, we had the practitioners select the most important factors, develop a causal model, and quantify their impact on effort overhead. Figure 3 shows the causal model developed in this study. The resulting model will be used in future evaluations at the company.

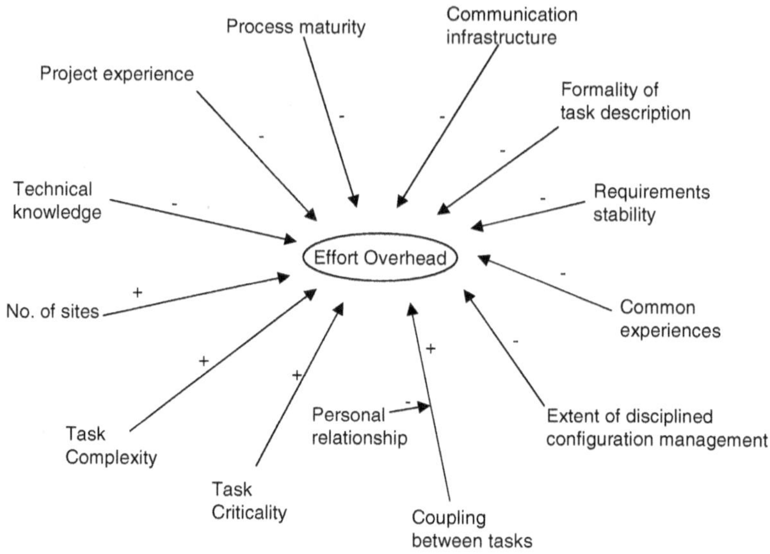

Fig. 3. Causal model for effort overhead

3.4 Integration of the Models

The three models described in the previous section have several commonalities: They all operate on a project management level and use the concept of influencing factors that impact the outcomes of a global software development project. However, at the same time, they all regard different perspectives and thus are important for making a systematic task assignment decision: The risk model can analyze existing and potential assignment alternatives with respect to project risks and problems in distributed development. Therefore it can not only support task assignment but also risk management for GSD projects. The assignment suggestion and the effort overhead model help identifying task assignment alternatives while considering multiple influencing factors and criteria.

As the task assignment and the effort overhead model both aim at the same goal, it could be argued to use only one of the models for task allocation. However, we see both of them as important: One the one hand, a systematic task allocation process should be able to regard multiple goals and measures (e.g., cost, time, or quality – but also other goals such as workforce motivation) which can only be ensured by a generic task assignment model. On the other hand, effort and productivity are a central aspect in software project management and effort models are well-known in software development practice and research [26] [5]. These models should be adapted to GSD and integrated into task allocation, as done in the effort overhead model.

As all models have influencing factors and causal relationships in common and should be used for a systematic task allocation process, we integrated them into one approach for systematic task allocation. This was mainly done following two principles:

1. The models are built on each other: Both the assignment suggestion and effort overhead model use the results of the risk model development as input for their underlying causal models. The risk model can be derived easily from lessons learned as it operates on a textual basis. During risk model development, influencing factors, goals, and causal relationships are identified. These are enhanced into a causal model that is the basis for the other two models. In addition, the weights identified during the assignment suggestion model development are the foundation for the quantification of the effort overhead model.

2. The assignment selection is done from different perspectives: The task allocation is done based on the suggestions made by the assignment suggestion and effort overhead model. This assignment is then analyzed using the risk model, ensuring that the task assignment decision is done systematically and regarding multiple perspectives.

In the following, the assignment selection process is described in detail.

3.5 Assignment Selection Process

Figure 4 gives an overview of the assignment selection process. In short, it consists of the development and application of the three sub-models in sequential order. In the following, we will explain all steps of the process.

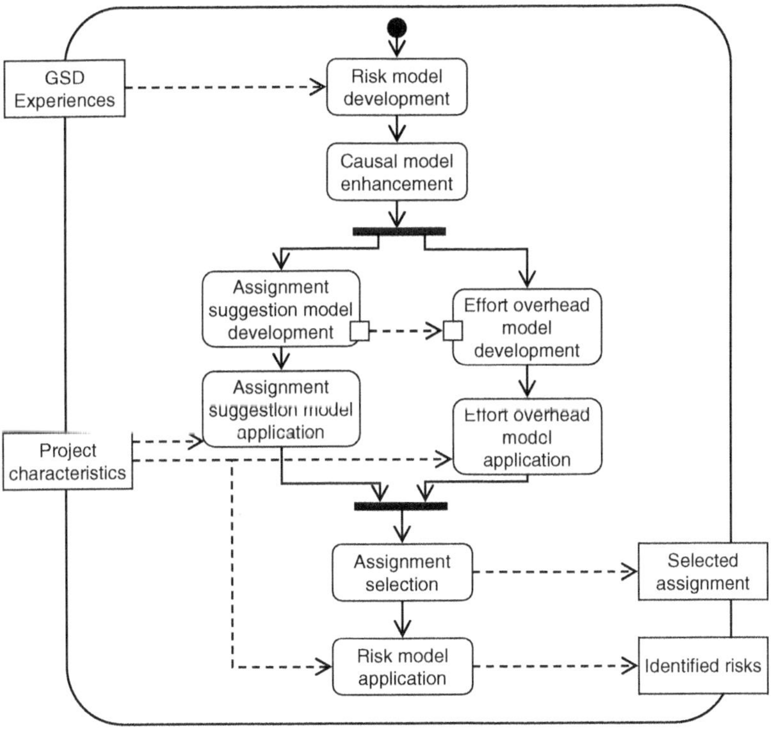

Fig. 4. Assignment selection process

1. Risk model development: The risk model is developed based on the experiences from past projects. By analyzing problems in previous GSD projects, their underlying causes, and their impact on project goals, rules are formulated as lessons learned that describe how project characteristics (i.e., influencing factors) impact the project. The influencing factors are categorized into different categories (e.g., characteristics of sites, relationships between sites).

Input: Experiences from past projects (e.g., lessons learned, expert interviews).
Output: Risk model; criteria for task allocation, risks, influencing factors, and causal relationships.

2. Causal model enhancement: The criteria, risks, influencing factors, and causal relationships identified in the risk model are refined into a causal model. This is done according to the following rules: First, all criteria and risks are linked to project goals by inserting new goals (e.g., cost minimization, workforce motivation, and product quality) and causal relationships. This ensures that for every influencing factor, the impact on project goals is described in the model. Second, new influencing factors are added that might not have been relevant in the risk model. This is done by checking for every goal in the causal model if all relevant influencing factors that might impact the goal are already included.

Input: Criteria for task allocation, risks, influencing factors, and causal relationships; expert estimations.
Output: Causal model.

3. Assignment suggestion model development: The causal model is refined into a Bayesian network model. In order to do so, the causal relationships have to be weighted and further specified. This has to be done using the estimation of experienced practitioners. The Bayesian network models can be automatically transferred into the assignment suggestion model using the TAMRI approach [10] [11].

Input: Causal model; expert estimations.
Output: Assignment suggestion model, weights on causal relationships.

4. Effort overhead model development: The effort overhead model is developed using the CoBRA methodology. For this, the causal model is used as input (however, only those factors and causal relationships that affect productivity). The weights of the Bayesian networks can be indicators for quantifying the impact.

Input: Causal model; weights on causal relationships; expert estimations.
Output: Effort overhead model.

5. Assignment suggestion model application: The assignment suggestion model is executed using the project (i.e., task, site, and general project) characteristics and project-specific weights on the assignment criteria as input. As a result, the model returns an ordered (with respect to the weighted criteria) list of assignment suggestions.

Input: Assignment suggestion model; project characteristics.
Output: List of assignment suggestions (1).

6. Effort overhead model application: Possible task assignments are analyzed using the effort overhead model. It returns effort estimations for each alternative, thus making it possible to order the alternatives based on the expected effort.

Input: Effort overhead model; project characteristics.
Output: List of assignment suggestions (2).

7. Assignment selection: The two lists of the effort overhead model and the assignment suggestion model might suggest different assignment alternatives, as they regard different viewpoints. Thus, the responsible project manager has to decide between both suggestions while keeping in mind that the effort overhead model solely regards productivity, while the assignment suggestion model considers multiple criteria but might be less accurate.

Input: List of assignment suggestions (1); list of assignment suggestions (2).
Output: Selected assignment.

8. Risk model application: The risk model can identify GSD-related project risks individually for a given project and task allocation decision. As the impact of influencing factors on project risks was refined in the two other models, it was used indirectly as basis for the task allocation decision. Thus, there is no need to apply the risk model in addition to the other models for making the task allocation decision. However, it should be applied as a final step in order to analyze the project risks for the selected task allocation. As a result, it returns a list of individual project risks that can be used for enacting countermeasures.

Input: Selected assignment; risk model; project characteristics.
Output: Identified project-specific risks.

4 Application Scenario

In the following, we will demonstrate the use of the approach by using an example scenario. In order to point out the relevant characteristics, we focus the scenario on relevant aspects and omit some details that are not relevant.

In the scenario, three components (A, B, and C) are to be developed and three sites are available (located in Germany, UK, and India). Due to project constraints, A has to be developed at the German site. B and C can now either be developed at the UK or at the Indian site. The Indian site has more expertise in working on component C and a generally lower labor cost rate. Figure 5 gives an overview of the scenario.

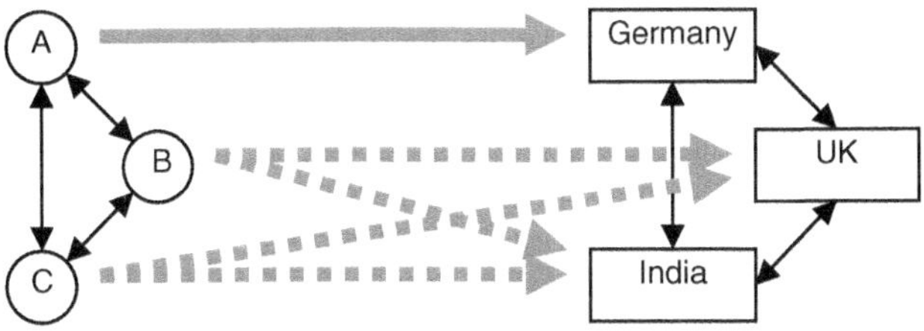

Fig. 5. Application scenario

The process steps of the approach will be applied as follows:

Step 1: A risk model is developed based on previous experiences. It results in three rules (in reality the set of rules might be significantly larger), which are demonstrated in Table 2.

Table 2. Risk model

Influencing factors	Rule	Textual description
Cultural differences, process maturity	Cultural differences and no process maturity → - productivity	Cultural differences between sites can reduce productivity if process maturity at the sites is not very high
Cultural differences	Cultural differences → - motivation	Cultural differences reduce workforce motivation
Expertise	Expertise → +productivity	Low expertise results in rework and thus reduces productivity

Step 2: The risk model is refined into a causal model. The experts name as project goals development costs (influenced by productivity), and workforce motivation. Further analysis reveals that workforce motivation is not only dependent on cultural differences but also on a site-specific motivation level. Thus, this is added as an influencing factor. Likewise, expertise is added as a factor influencing productivity.

Step 3: The Bayesian networks are built out of the causal model. Figure 6 gives an excerpt of the Bayesian networks together with the relative weights.

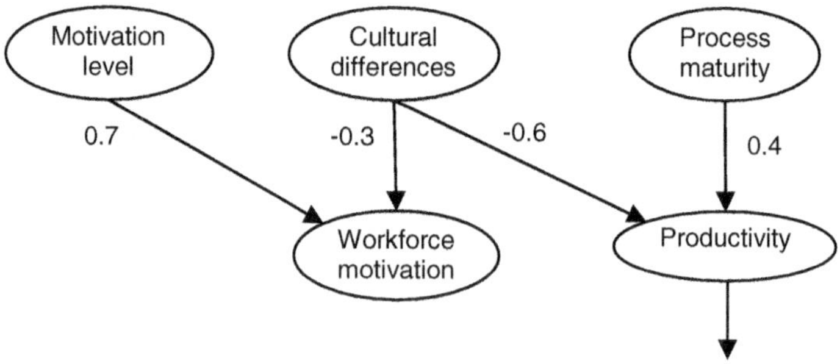

Fig. 6. Bayesian network excerpt

Step 4: For the effort overhead model, only the influences on productivity are regarded. This means that the impact of cultural differences on workforce motivation is left out. Figure 7 shows the resulting causal model.

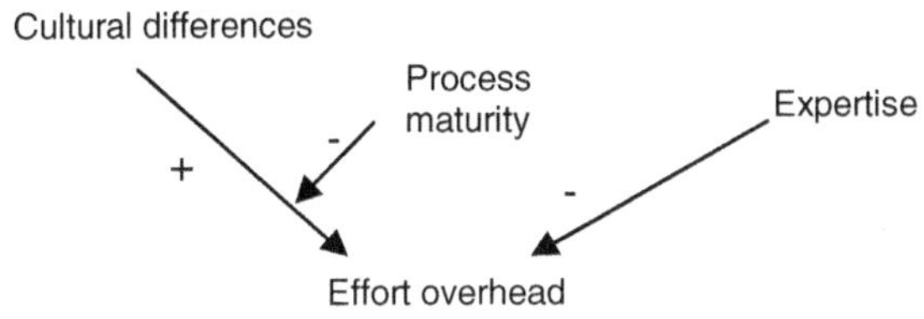

Fig. 7. Causal model for effort overhead

Step 5: The project characteristics are inserted into the assignment suggestion model. For the concrete example, this means, for instance, that the cultural differences between the UK and Germany are relatively low, while the differences between Germany and India are high. In addition, the weights on the assignment goals are set. In this scenario, keeping the workforce motivated is less important than achieving high productivity. Consequently, the model suggests assigning component C to India (due to the higher expertise) but assigning B to the UK site due to the lower cultural differences to Germany.

Step 6: Using the effort overhead model, the development costs for each assignment alternative are estimated. In this scenario, the cultural differences between India and Europe lead to only a minor productivity drop due to relatively high process maturity. Thus, the model suggests assigning B and C to India in order to profit from the lower labor cost rates.

Step 7: The project manager now has to decide between the different suggestions of the models. As both models suggest assigning C to India, it remains to be decided whether B should be assigned to the UK or to India. Finally, the project manager decides to assign B to the UK.

Step 8: The resulting assignment is: A → Germany, B → UK, and C → India. This is then analyzed using the rules of the risk model. The risk model predicts that the cultural differences between India and UK/Germany might cause low motivation among the workforce. Now, the project manager will be able to enact countermeasures such as initiating personal contacts between workers in India and Germany/UK.

5 Conclusion and Future Work

In this article, we presented an approach for systematic task allocation evaluation in global software development that consists of three sub-models, each regarding task allocation from a different perspective, interfaces between these models, and a decision process that uses all three models in sequential order.

While the individual models have already been published and have also been evaluated in an industrial context, we have now integrated them into one coherent approach. The advantage is that, on the one hand, weaknesses of the individual models can be eliminated. For example, the effort overhead model is not able to take into account criteria other than overall effort and total development costs (however, the assignment suggestion model and risk model are) and the risk model is not able to evaluate a large set of assignment alternatives (which is possible using the other two models). On the other hand, the underlying concepts such as influencing factors and causal relationships can be reused between the different models. This reduces the effort for developing the other two models once one model has been developed.

However, there are still some limitations to this approach: Even though we tried to eliminate this threat by using multiple models, the impact of a task assignment decision is often influenced by many different influencing factors and criteria that are often very hard to collect and even harder to weight or quantify. Therefore, the final decision cannot be made by decision models but rather has to be made by experienced project managers. This was also a reason for us to include a manual assignment selection step in the process (step 7): The models only deliver weighted lists of assignment suggestions to help the decision maker; the final decision, however, is made by the responsible manager (this manual selection might not scale up with big projects and very large numbers of tasks but in the industrial projects we analyzed, only a limited number of tasks was freely assignable to the available sites). In general, we think that the use of our approach can help make the decision more systematic and can support the manager in making a decision that is based on aggregated organizational experience (thus making the quality of the decision less dependant on the individual expertise of the manager).

Another limitation is the fact that the approach assumes the existence of very specific knowledge at a certain point in the project (e.g., at project start or after high-level design): The project manager must be able to divide the work into distinct tasks and name the characteristics of the tasks, the available sites, and the overall project. This might not be possible in every project and also implies some restrictions for software development processes. For example, in a completely agile process the characteristics of the tasks might not be known, thus hindering the use of this approach. However, we think that for a systematic task allocation decision, this information has to be available independent of the use of this approach. We thus see this rather as a limitation of systematic task allocation in general than of this specific approach.

A further limitation might be the effort needed to develop and maintain these models. Especially creating a Bayesian network can be very costly. However, in the TAMRI approach, we used some simple mathematical formulas (e.g., calculating the weighted average value of two inputs) for creating the probabilistic tables of the networks which largely reduced the effort. In addition, we believe that a systematic task allocation decision can reduce the overhead in distributed development projects by a much larger amount than the additional effort for the model development and application. Furthermore, the models and Bayesian networks can be reused in between projects. In future work, we will concentrate on methods for systematically reusing the models and including feedback of project managers.

In further future work, we will evaluate the approach in a real industrial context (as already done with the risk model). This will result in much more complex model instances as shown in the example: The prototype risk model developed in an industrial context consisted of 36 rules instead of 3. The assignment suggestion model contained two Bayesian networks with 14 and 16 nodes, and the effort overhead model contained 14 effort drivers. In further future work, we will investigate other interdependencies between the models. For example, the results of the cost overhead model development (i.e., the quantification of the effort overhead drivers) could be used as input for developing the assignment suggestion model.

In addition, we are planning to implement the models together with the integration process as one task allocation support tool. Individual tools have already been implemented: A prototype of the risk model has been implemented using Microsoft Excel. The assignment suggestion model has been implemented as an extensible Java tool with its own graphical user interface [11]. For the effort overhead model, there exists a general implementation of the CoBRA approach as well as an Excel model for evaluating task allocation alternatives [13]. However, a coherent implementation that integrates all models is missing yet.

Another area of future work is the integration of the models in risk management approaches. The risk model already is able to name some GSD-specific risks. However, other aspects of risk management are not supported yet: The probability of meeting certain predefined project goals (e.g. cost, time, quality) cannot be assed using the current model specification. However, the standard CoBRA approach is able to do so by using simulation. In future work, we want to integrate this into our assignment suggestion and effort overhead model.

Acknowledgment

The authors would like to thank Sonnhild Namingha for proofreading this paper.

References

1. Grinter, R.E., Herbsleb, J.D., Perry, D.E.: The geography of coordination: Dealing with Distance in R&D Work. In: Proc. ACM Conference on Supporting Group Work (GROUP 1999), pp. 306–315 (1999)
2. Mockus, A., Weiss, D.M.: Globalization by Chunking: A Quantitative Approach. IEEE Software 18(2), 30–37 (2001)
3. Lamersdorf, A., Münch, J., Rombach, D.: A survey on the state of the practice in distributed software development: Criteria for task allocation. In: Proceedings Fourth International Conference on Global Software Engineering, pp. 41–50 (2009)
4. Bass, M., Paulish, D.: Global Software Development Process Research at Siemens. In: Third International Workshop on Global Software Development (2004)
5. Keil, P., Paulish, D.J., Sangwan, R.: Cost Estimation for Global Software Development. In: International Workshop on Economics Driven Software Engineering, Shanghai, China, pp. 7–10 (2006)
6. Herbsleb, J.D., Mockus, A.: An Empirical Study of Speed and Communication in Globally-Distributed Software Development. IEEE Transactions on Software Engineering 29(6), 481–494 (2003)
7. Smite, D., Moe, N.B.: Understanding a Lack of Trust in Global Software Teams: A Multiple-Case Study. In: Münch, J., Abrahamsson, P. (eds.) PROFES 2007. LNCS, vol. 4589, pp. 20–34. Springer, Heidelberg (2007)
8. Carmel, E., Abbott, P.: Why 'nearshore' means that distance matters. Communications of the ACM 50(10), 40–46 (2007)

9. Palmer, J., Speier, C., Buckley, M., Moore, J.E.: Recruiting and retaining IS personnel: factors influencing employee turnover. In: ACM SIGCPR Conference on Computer Personnel Research, pp. 286–288 (1998)
10. Lamersdorf, A., Münch, J., Rombach, H.D.: A Decision Model for Supporting Task Allocation Processes in Global Software Development. In: PROFES 2009, LNBIP, vol. 32, pp. 332–346. Springer, Heidelberg (2009)
11. Lamersdorf, A., Münch, J.: TAMRI: A Tool for Supporting Task Distribution in Global Software Development Projects. In: International Workshop on Tool Support Development and Management in Distributed Software Projects, collocated with the IEEE International Conference on Global Software Engineering, ICGSE 2009, pp. 322–327 (2009)
12. Lamersdorf, A., Münch, J.: Studying the Impact of Global Software Development Characteristics on Project Goals: A Causal Model. The Open Software Engineering Journal (accepted for publication)
13. Münch, J., Lamersdorf, A.: Systematic Task Allocation Evaluation in Distributed Software Development. In: Meersman, R., Herrero, P., Dillon, T. (eds.) OTM 2009 Workshops. LNCS, vol. 5872, pp. 228–237. Springer, Heidelberg (2009)
14. Lamersdorf, A., Münch, J., Rombach, H.D.: Towards a Multi-criteria Development Distribution Model: An Analysis of Existing Task Distribution Approaches. In: Third IEEE International Conference on Global Software Development, pp. 109–118 (2008)
15. Edwards, H.K., Kim, J.H., Park, S., Al-Ani, B.: Global Software Development: Project Decomposition and Task Allocation. In: International Conference on Business and Information (2008)
16. Setamanit, S., Wakeland, W.W., Raffo, D.: Planning and Improving Global Software Development Process Using Simulation. In: International Workshop on Global Software Development for the Practitioner (2006)
17. Setamanit, S., Wakeland, W.W., Raffo, D.: Using simulation to evaluate global software development task allocation strategies. Software Process: Improvement and Practice 12(5), 491–503 (2007)
18. Sooraj, P., Mohapatra, P.K.J.: Developing an Inter-site Coordination Index for Global Software Development. In: International IEEE Conference on Global Software Engineering, pp. 119–128 (2008)
19. Raghvinder, S., Bass, M., Mullick, N., Paulish, D.J., Kazmeier, J.: Global Software Development Handbook. Auerbach Publications, London (2006)
20. Prikladnicki, R., Audy, J.L.N., Evaristo, R.: A Reference Model for Global Software Development: Findings from a Case Study. In: International IEEE Conference on Global Software Engineering, pp. 18–28 (2006)
21. Ralyte, J., Lamielle, X., Arni-Bloch, N., Leonard, M.: A Framework for Supporting Management in Distributed Information Systems Development. In: Second International Conference on Research Challenges in Information Science, pp. 381–392 (2008)
22. Ebert, C., Murthy, B.K., Jha, N.N.: Managing Risks in Global Software Engineering: Principles and Practices. In: International Conference on Global Software Engineering, pp. 131–140 (2008)
23. Smite, D.: Project Outcome Predictions: Risk Barometer Based on Historical Data. In: International IEEE Conference on Global Software Engineering, pp. 103–112 (2007)
24. Boehm, B., Abts, C., Brown, A., Chulani, S., Clark, B., Horowitz, E., Madachy, R., Reifer, D., Steece, B.: Software Cost Estimation with COCOMO II. Prentice-Hall, Englewood Cliffs (2000)

25. Betz, S., Mäkiö, J.: Amplification of the COCOMO II regarding Offshore Software Projects. In: Workshop on Offshoring of Software Development-Methods and Tools for Risk Management at the Second International Conference on Global Software Engineering (2007)
26. Madachy, R.: Distributed Global Development Parametric Cost Modeling. In: Wang, Q., Pfahl, D., Raffo, D.M. (eds.) ICSP 2007. LNCS, vol. 4470, pp. 159–168. Springer, Heidelberg (2007)
27. Fenton, N., Marsh, W., Neil, M., Cates, P., Forey, S., Tailor, M.: Making Resource Decisions for Software Projects. In: International Conference on Software Engineering, pp. 397–406 (2004)
28. Briand, L.C., El Emam, K., Bomarius, F.: COBRA: A Hybrid Method for Software Cost Estimation, Benchmarking, and Risk Assessment. In: International Conference on Software Engineering, pp. 390–399 (1998)
29. Trendowicz, A., Heidrich, J., Münch, J., Ishigai, Y., Yokoyama, K., Kikuchi, N.: Development of a Hybrid Cost Estimation Model in an Iterative Manner. In: International Conference on Software Engineering, pp. 331–340 (2006)

The Economics of Hiring and Staff Retention for an IT Company in Russia

Andrey Terekhov[1] and Karina Terekhova[2]

[1] Saint-Petersburg State University, Lanit-Tercom – Universitetsky 28, Peterhof, Saint-Petersburg, Russia
andrey.terekhov@lanit-tercom.com
[2] Nokia OY, Helsinki, Finland
karina.terekhov@nokia.com

Abstract. Two different approaches to the the economics of hiring and staff retention for an IT company in Russia are presented. 10-year experience of successful collaboration between Saint-Petersburg State University and software company Lanit-Tercom is shown. In the course of this collaboration Lanit-Tercom employees work as tutors with University students, supervising their diploma and other scientific works.

The enterprise allocates a relatively big budget for this purpose and nevertheless, if one compares these expenses with traditional HR processes (hiring, retraining, etc), taking into account the average duration of employment of the staff, the described approach is more preferable. In justification of this conclusion, calculations and arguments are presented in the article.

Keywords: software industry, economics of hiring and staff retention, training and retraining, new method of industrial education, project managers' education.

1 Introduction

One of the biggest problems of the IT industry in Russia today is lack of human resources.

All sorts of educational institutions in Russia are straining to train software engineers, software testers, software project managers and IT system integrators. Among the institutions are the established universities with long-standing traditions in the field, as well as polytechnics and private SW training courses.

The gap in IT workforce is still big (see [1]).

Some ten or fifteen years ago the lack of SW development resources in Russia was commonly blamed on the brain drain towards the West. Now this is no longer the case – the brain drain to the West has all but stopped. The opposite trend can be observed – IT companies in Russia now list among their employees many Russian returners from abroad, as well as Russians brought up abroad returning to Russia.

The idea of further education of IT staff is also gaining in popularity. The majority of medium to large sized IT companies have established personnel training centers to help induction process or to enhance the SW skills of the newly recruited people. Additional training often increases the company overheads, but there is no other way to achieve people productivity.

M. Nordio et al. (Eds.): SEAFOOD 2010, LNBIP 54, pp. 54–63, 2010.

It is one thing when the skills that a new employee must get are just the induction into the company business and management processes, adopted technologies and customer culture. It is quite another proposition to teach programming languages or the basics of algorithm efficiency. In this case the quality of recruitment must be considered insufficient, since the new employee cannot reach full productivity in reasonable time.

According to the laws of the market, the deficit of supply causes growth of compensation offered to the recruits. Why relocate abroad when it is enough to change jobs to gain an increase in your salary? There is a lot in favour of staying in Russia– the personal tax is low (it is 13% in Russia), no language problems plus the quality of living became comparable to the West for the middle class. So why not swap jobs every couple of years – with a gain?

The problems accumulate for the employers. Whereas personal tax is low in Russia, the personnel tax for the enterprise is relatively high (26.2% of the person's salary) – to compare, the average percentage for European countries is 15%. The costs of premises, infrastructure and data costs are constantly growing despite hopeful forecasts. As a result it is expensive for an enterprise to hire people if they do not achieve productivity within a short time from start date. Unfortunately, this is most often the case.

The total output of Russian higher education streams producing new IT and SW specialists is in the area of 150 thousand graduates a year. This is among the highest numbers in the world, and the demand for the graduates is still higher. Besides, the quality of graduates varies a lot among the institutions, especially in small towns.

Another widespread problem in Russia is that the new graduates of higher education are not trained in the SW development management processes and in professional communication and teamwork skills. Other blank areas are SW development infrastructure skills – versioning and version control, work planning, reporting, testing and quality assurance, budgeting for time and money per unit of SW and so on. Some other institutions, on the contrary, are guilty of the too down to earth approach – teaching only specific technologies (such as .NET or SAP) without the fundamental knowledge base.

This means that every IT company in Russia must in any case spend money on identification, hiring and training of suitable personnel. In this article we compare two approaches to personnel hiring and retention in IT industry, and we will discuss the comparative costs and benefits of these approaches.

2 Profit Margins of SW Development Business in Russia

Any software business requires many well-qualified entry-level developers and testers (with work experience 0-2 years). In the organization chart they make up to half of the total production workforce. They usually are also the most mobile employees – turnover of the entry-level staff is higher than average. Entry-level developers and testers as a rule need more hours of induction training, too. So what is the bottom-line profitability of entry-level workforce for the company?

Lets assume the base salary level is $1000 (this is in the low range but realistic for inexperienced developers). The first overhead that the company pays is the Russian social tax (26.2%).

Both the potential candidates and the company customers are sensitive to the quality of company premises, so the next biggest cost item is rent and service of premises. At the moment of writing (second half of 2008) the cost of renting an average business space in an office building in St.Petersburg is $35 per sq meter. According to the Russian labour law, a company must allow at least10 sq meters per employee brutto (including a proportion of common spaces such as meeting rooms, bathrooms and coffee spaces). Therefore the company spends on average $350 per employee in premises rent.

Overheads per employee include also the service costs – administration, communications, technology and hardware. Service costs are typically calculated as 30% of base salary. We shall add $300 for service costs. Accounting standards usually calculate service costs together with the rent as "overheads", but in our case the cost of rent is growing faster than the service costs, so it makes sense to keep it separate.

To keep peace with the tax authorities, a company must show profits (otherwise it will be suspected of money laundering). In Russia the minimum profit for tax report is 10% of the annual turnover. To convert this minimum into the terms of our research, let us assume that it is evaluated as 20% of base salary per employee (which roughly denotes 10% of turnover). Therefore there will be nominal tax levied on $200 – in Russia the profit tax is 24%, which makes the total tax levied per employee $48.

Consolidating the expenses, we calculate the total overhead per one entry-level staff as:

$1000+$262+$350+$300+$48=**$1960 per month**

On the benefits side, the work of the same entry-level developer or tester can be invoiced as customer consultancy or development services at a price of at most $15 per hour at the current market prices. This makes $2400 per month (assuming 160 work hours to a calendar month). This is only the potential – given that this much work will be invoiced in fact.

Unfortunately, it is rare to find the efficiency of more than 85% per employee in an IT company. Sick leave, gaps in orders, training and similar issues take their toll. Therefore the total average profit per employee is:

$2400*0.85=$2040

Evidently, the profitability is low – only 4% (even less than the nominal $200 prescribed by tax authorities).

The only realistic way to improve the profitability is to sell the services of developers and testers to customers at more than the rock-bottom invoicing price of $15 by offering a better value of their work. This is, in fact, what the companies do, and they achieve the new customer value by training the employees and enhancing their work experience.

This calculation shows effectively that the entry-level staff retention and further training is a more important goal for an IT or SW company than hiring new entry-level workforce.

In the next chapter we shall consider the methods that the companies typically employ for hiring and retention, and we shall try to estimate their comparative success rate (defined as the length of employment in the same company of the newly hired entry-level staff).

3 Direct Costs of Recruitment in Today's Labour Market

We are concerned primarily with Russian market here, and maybe even more specifically – SW developer labour market in St.Petersburg.

There are approximately 25 universities and other higher education institutions that together yield about 4000 graduates annually with the B.Sc and M.Sc diplomas in SW engineering and related specializations (listed in the Russian Ministry of Education certified qualifications register under category "information and communication technologies").

The demand for such specialists is estimated to be ten times higher than this number. Ten years ago still many fewer graduates were produced each year, but this was partially balanced by the conversion of other specialists to SW development and information technologies skills under the pressure from the strong IT employment market (and the corresponding stagnation of other engineering employment market then).

Today the trend has changed, the industry in Russia is on the rise, and the retraining of other specialists to IT qualifications has all but stopped.

Large and very large companies enjoy the luxury of candidates seeking employment there without extra effort of the company part. However, the free-flowing stream is not usually enough (and not enough of the right kind for the moment), so even the big corporation allocate budget for recruitment costs. Every successfully recruited candidate costs the company 15-20% of the annual base salary – to be paid to the hiring agency. In our case this is $3000 - $4000.

Let us assume that the basic skills are already there (such as SW coding in the right language, knowledge of technology and algorithms). This leaves the need for company processes and management training, SW version control, training in the specific SW development tools used by the company. In addition, there is the induction period when the new employee is introduced to the specifications, requirements and the code produced for the project/projects that the person will participate.

In short – there is always the need for induction training, and the need is always extensive.

According to different schools of thought, the total "time to productivity" for a new SW developer or tester in a company lies between 1,5 and 3 months (this costs the company between $3000 and $4000). This is an underestimate, because in some cases there are also additional third party course training required (another $1000 - $2000), and the established staff spends time to carry out the induction with the new employee (estimated $1000 to $2000). Sometimes the whole process lasts longer than three months.

However, accounting for all probabilities, we get the costs of induction to be somewhere between $8000 and $14000 per employee.

If all goes well, the entry-level developer or tester gets a promotion in one or two years (after participating in one or two successful projects), and to replace him or her recruitment must start again. Therefore, the company should aim to recoup the initial costs of recruitment within two years maximum.

As the calculated profit margin of an entry-level employee is only 4% (see chapter 2) and average monthly sales $2040, the annual profit per employee does not exceed $1000 ($2040 * 12 *0.04). This makes it clear that it is hardly possible to recoup even the minimal initial recruitment costs in two years.

This leads to a natural question – why do the companies go for the expenses and trouble if it does not pay in the end?

The first reason is the production volumes – to keep orders coming in, the company must show excess capacity and ability for sustainable growth as needed.

The other, less obvious reason is to do with retention. If staff retention in the company is high, then the company can plan for higher profits generated by this employee later.

In any case, the new hiring cycle must repeat every year, and there is a strong economical incentive to carry it out as efficient as possible. IT companies in Russia (as well as in Europe in general) aim to carry out recruitment at costs not exceeding the industry average (which in 2009 for IT and telecom industry in Europe was on the level of €5050 per new recruitment, see [3]).

4 Our Approach to Recruitment

In the earlier chapters we have demonstrated that recruitment of entry-level specialists is a tough task and that the associated costs can easily outweigh the benefits. Are there any alternative approaches which may help to make it a more repeatable and profitable process?

Since one of the authors combines work in business with heading the chair of SW engineering in St.Petersburg State University, his thinking was naturally directed towards involving the companies in the teaching process and reaping the benefits from student participation in real-life projects.

The idea is not new and not unique. Industry-funded chairs operated in universities and other higher education institutions still in the USSR times. At those times, in absence of market economy conditions, the cost of training a specialist was not accounted in the same way that we do now. The collaboration was prescribed by the plan, which overruled economic considerations then.

Today many companies support higher education by distributing student grants, research and teaching grants, as well as supplying the equipment, licenses and project costs of teaching and research. All of this helps and at the same time – this type of support is not systematic and does not noticeably influence either the quality of training or the likelihood of the graduates to choose the sponsor company as their first employment.

In some cases that we know a company established a full-blown further education course in collaboration with a university. Almost in all cases the students had to pay themselves for the course – this means that the company in question aimed not only at improving their recruitment prospects, but also meant it to be a profitable business enterprise.

All such attempts that we are aware of have failed due to financial reasons.

Thus a straightforward business idea of training your own workforce when still in education turns out to be tricky in the details of implementation. No surprise that it was not warmly received when proposed to the management team of Lanit-Tercom (company that the first author headed at the time). Indeed, why solve the problems of higher education at the expense of a particular business? What is the motivation for the employees to participate in teaching process?

The answer is that the benefits are mutual. For the university it is in the quality of the graduates, in the recruitment index and the ratings of the chair among the best employers. For the sponsor company it makes the recruitment almost foolproof and radically cuts the induction costs for the new employees.

Put this way – this is an attractive proposition. So it also turned in practice, after a period of trial and error and process adjustment. Lanit-Tercom and faculty of mathematics and mechanics of St.Petersburg State University succeeded in implementing a practical teaching process putting all students through participation in real-life SW development projects, and recruiting 20 to 25 people annually to Lanit-Tercom directly after graduation. The costs of recruitment and induction dropped, and the retention of employees recruited in this way is higher than average retention in the company.

The collaboration was started almost ten years ago and continues now with the stable rates of success.

Here we shall capture the main points of our approach that were operational in creating the success story. We think that similar collaboration can be reproduced with equal measure of success if certain basic conditions are met.

First of all, the education partner in collaboration must teach a firm foundation of courses in mathematics and in information sciences. Theoretical basis is essential for high-quality SW engineers, and no amount of work experience can replace it.

It helps if the program includes the SW project management disciplines reflecting the state or art in current processes (adopted by the companies not only locally, but international, too). Whereas Russian higher education is traditionally strong in theoretical subjects and teaching the classical art of programming and testing – it is less strong in practical disciplines related to SW production.

The task is made easier if the university (or other higher education partner in collaboration) follows the international standards in teaching, such as Computer Science Curricula 2001 or Software Engineering Curricula 2004. For example, these standards were translated into Russian and adopted for teaching in the faculty of mathematics and mechanics of St.Petersburg State University since 2001.

What is the role of the collaborating company partner? Briefly – inviting students in on SW development project participation and spending time in developing their communication and process skills. This is how it happens, stage by stage.

By any standards of higher education, Russian or international, SW engineering students must do some research work in their third and subsequent years of education. In addition, M.Sc. students also produce their master thesis in their final year.

The collaborating company can participate actively in all these activities by:

- Appointing supervisors selected among the experienced project or team leaders who will take care of individual student's practice
- Appointing group tutors who will supervise group project participation (recommended by the above mentioned SW Engineering Curricula)
- Supplying the process framework and the necessary equipment for students' participation in SW development projects
- Providing timely and accurate feedback on each student's project work to the faculty
- Supply teaching some of the newer subjects in SW engineering if the faculty staff cannot cover the topics yet

To sum up, the third requirement towards successful collaboration is the readiness of the company to commit to the tasks listed above.

Apart from the money issues, two main questions must be resolved by the partners before entering the collaboration:

- How close are the technologies and algorithms developed in the company to the profile of the teaching partner? Will there be sufficient scope for the students to implement in the projects the disciplines they are taught?

– This issue must be addressed by careful selection of collaboration partners.

- What is the guarantee of success? What if the company spends time and money on student training, and the students apply to other employers after graduation?

– In our practice this is a surprisingly low risk. The issue is close to the problem of retention, and the same rules apply – good conditions and emotional commitment created by individual attention ensure that the majority of students are willing to consider employment in the collaborating company.

The commitment created at the first recruitment continues in high retention figures during employment. Our numbers show that on average an employee recruited to the company via this process stays with the company almost twice as long as an employee hired in the usual way.

5 How Does It Work in Practice?

Let us take for example Lanit-Tercom budget for collaboration expenses in academic year 2007/2008 (before crisys). We shall start with a detailed description of the company participation in teaching process, so that the items of budgeting make sense.

One of the key methods to engage the students initially in the SW development project and processes is to conduct regular seminar-type workshops led by the experienced project managers from the company. Students from the informatics stream of the faculty, as well as other students from the same faculty (and sometimes even from other departments or institutions) attend these seminars. All attendees are divided into relatively small groups (5-10 people in each). At this stage no selection or restrictions to attendance are in place.

The seminars are part of regular workload for Lanit-Tercom employees who volunteer to lead them. The company aims at finding volunteer leaders from each company department, so that they cover maximally large areas of IT technology expertise present in Lanit-Tercom. Thanks to the wide coverage, most students find an area that interests them best, and start to dig deeper.

Each group works according to a common learning plan. At the beginning of year the leader holds a few sessions of "induction" to develop the background knowledge about the SW production process and tools and practices used in it. At the same time the induction sessions help to bind the group together, to start acting as a team. The leader and students have time to discuss the proposed project briefs, and to make a guided choice for each student- which project he or she will join.

Then the project phase starts. Each project is led by at least two Lanit-Tercom employees to ensure continuity of guidance in case of absences (business trips, deadlines, sick leave). As a rule projects last for three months.

The topics for the projects are selected by the faculty members and by Lanit-Tercom student group leaders together, in close discussion. The final list of topics is approved by the chair of SW engineering, evaluating both the theoretical value and whether the project will fit into the curriculum. Under these conditions, the projects can be submitted to the faculty as the official yearly project (of course if it was completed before the deadline).

Each topic makes a joint project work for several students as a team. This is a must if the aim is to develop the skills of large-scale SW development. It is interesting to note that we do not appoint project leaders from the students – they come up naturally in team interaction.

When a project is completed, the project team makes project presentation for an approval review. During the review, every project team member must tell about their part of work and their understanding of the results and process. We evaluate not only the content of presentation but also the presentation skills.

For the best students, selected from all project teams, we offer the possibility of a summer school during the university vacations. Summer school consists of four hours training a day for a month. Lanit-Tercom pays a small stipend to summer school participants, including bonuses paid for the best participation.

For example, in 2007-2008 we formed nine student project groups, counting 80 participants in total. By the time the projects have finished 60 students remained committed. This is considered a success – at the beginning, in earlier years of collaboration, the final count was often less than a half of the starting count. The improvement is due to the better choice of project subjects and the steep learning curve that both the faculty and Lanit-Tercom took in organizing this type of collaboration.

6 How Much Does It Cost to the Company?

Each Lanit-Tercom employee participating in the scheme is paid a small bonus ($100-$200) in compensation of approximately six hours a week workload. These six hours come from the normal working schedule, so that the productive work suffers as a result to some extent. The company accepts this as part of the deal in getting better workforce in future.

In the year 2007/2008 Lanit-Tercom spent $30000 for the student projects and teaching, and 30 new graduates were recruited in the same year (each recruitment cost approximately $1000 to the company). It is true that the needs for induction and additional training apply also in the case of hiring the students who went through the practice process, but the resulting quality is reliably high. Most of the current department heads and team leades in Lanit-Tercom were originally recruited via the same process.

However, the total need for workforce in Lanit-Tercom is bigger than what this process brings to the company. Besides, in some cases specialists in areas that we do not teach ourselves are needed. This is why Lanit-Tercom HR service is also actively recruiting. For example, in the same year 2007/2008 20 people were hired to the company in the usual way. Therefore we have material for comparison of both traditional and customized recruitment.

7 Implications to Staff Retention

It is hardly surprising that the HR studies list compensation as the most important factor of staf retention in a company. Staff surveys at Lanit-Tercom confirm that this is indeed a strong priority for most employees.

Having said that, here is the full list of retention factors, consistently named by Lanit-Tercom staff:

1. Large stable company with comparatively long standing in the area
2. Close links to St.Petersburg State University, specialization in high technology projects
3. Diversity in product and service lines, opportunities to gain expertise in various subjects and technologies
4. CMM certification ensuring efficient management and established production processes
5. Competitive salary
6. Other forms of compensation:

   - Private medical insurance paid by the company
   - Free foreign language lessons for the employees
   - Fully official salary and fulfilling other trade union requirements
   - Corporate entertainment

Gathering and utilizing insight on the real priorities for people, measuring the relative impact of changes in each of the retention factors, and applying the knowledge to our people strategies – all these has helped Lanit-Tercom to reduce staff turnover from 12% five years ago to just 8%.

Our findings confirm that even in the employee market the people do not leave a company because the grass is greener somewhere else – but because it is "not green enough" in the place they are leaving. Other companies in IT market in Russia confirm the hypothesis and look for innovative approaches to recruitment and staff retention – even the big players lack personnel (see for example the survey in [2]).

The retention index for a particular employee consists of compensation and non-monetary factors. It is clear that the compensation package is the same (or close enough) for all newly recruited employees – whatever the method of their recruitment. If there are differences in average retention length for people hired in the traditional way (via agencies and advertisement) and hired via the academic collaboration program – these differences must be explained by non-monetary reasons.

This is what we see in practice. As already mentioned, on average the employees recruited through the academic collaboration scheme stay with the company up to double the time compared to people recruited in other ways. We are justified in assuming that the reasons like collaboration with the university, technology-intensive production processes, and especially –familiar product and business processes play an important role in these people's motivation to stay.

8 Conclusions

This article dealt with the economics of recruiting entry-level staff to an IT company in Russia, given the conditions of undersaturated labour market.

We demonstrated that the traditional recruitment with the help of agencies and advertisement results in high initial costs of hiring and induction, which may not be easily offset by profits if the turnover is relatively high in the company. Even with the typical international statistics of retention in IT area (3-4 years in the same place) it may be hard to break even when recruiting entry-level staff.

It is also dangerously easy to slip in quality of induction when balancing the costs of recruitment.

On the other hand, collaboration between IT companies and academic institutions of higher education looks favourable and mutually beneficial. Viewed as a method of recruitment, it can bring a steady flow of applications to entry-level positions and at the same time – reduce the budget for induction and training by shifting a large part of training earlier, to the time when students participate in collaboration program.

Certain conditions, described in chapter 4 of the paper, ensure the success of collaboration for both academic and industry partner.

We analyzed the example of a long standing collaboration between St.Petersburg State University and Lanit-Tercom and calculated the budget allocated by the company for the purposes of student training.

In addition, recruitment via the collaboration program has been shown as an efficient retention mechanism, helping to increase loyalty in the newly-hired employees. The increase in loyalty is due to the factors that are strongly improved with the prehire training – and their priority and validity are confirmed by the employees rating them in anonymous surveys.

We hope that the intent of this paper will be fulfilled if more companies operating in IT field in Russia prove the feasibility of collaboration with academic institutions by creating more success stories of their own in a similar way.

References

1. Bakanova, A.: Staffing crisis in IT: recruitment requirements slip (in Russian: Кадровый кризис в ИТ: планка требований сбита). Information Security (October 2007), http://www.itsec.ru/articles2/Inf_security/kadrovy-crisys
2. Survey on IT personnel recruitment and development on the recruitment site "Workjob.ru" (experts comments), http://www.workjob.ru/tech/personnel/206/
3. European recruitment costs per industry, UniversumQuarterly, IT and telecom, http://www.employerbrandingtoday.com/fi/2009/07/02/cost-per-hire-are-you-spending-more-money-than-your-competitors/#more-119

Global Software Project Management: A Case Study

Petra Björndal[1], Karen Smiley[2], and Prateeti Mohapatra[3]

[1] ABB Corporate Research, Industrial Software Systems
Forskargränd 7, 721 78 Västerås, Sweden
petra.bjorndal@se.abb.com
[2] ABB Corporate Research, Industrial Software Systems
940 Main Campus Drive, Raleigh, NC, 27606 United States
karen.smiley@us.abb.com
[3] ABB Corporate Research, Industrial Software Systems
Whitefield Road, 560048 Bangalore, Karnataka, India
prateeti.mohapatra@in.abb.com

Abstract. Global software development (GSD) is a growing phenomenon in industry, including the ABB Group of companies, which has a long history of executing globally distributed development projects. Geographic and temporal separation, culturally-based misunderstandings, and language effects are well-described complications for GSD teams. These factors aggravate issues (on both a practical and a leadership level) in communication, trust, and coordination, impeding the effective sharing and management of team knowledge, and creating risks to project success. In the interest of continually improving our business performance, ABB has joined the research community in exploring these issues and ways to increase awareness and tactical support for GSD project managers. In this paper, we present aggregate findings from qualitative interviews with people across different sites in the organization, and describe how identifying, measuring, and actively managing GSD-related risks can help project managers and leaders in planning and executing projects more effectively.

Keywords: offshore, management, risk, measurement, collaboration.

1 Introduction

The ABB Group of companies (www.abb.com) is a world leader in power and automation technologies, and many ABB products involve software components developed by globally distributed software development (GSD) teams, making high-quality GSD project performance a key concern. In the interest of continually improving our business performance, ABB has joined the research community in exploring these issues and ways to increase awareness and tactical support for GSD project managers.

In this paper, we present findings from a formative case study of seven GSD projects. Based on qualitative interviews and questionnaires, we explore the particular challenges associated with the project manager role in GSD. Our purpose is to increase business performance: by providing deeper insight into the specific challenges

M. Nordio et al. (Eds.): SEAFOOD 2010, LNBIP 54, pp. 64–70, 2010.

associated with GSD projects, and by actively focusing on giving risk management guidance to project managers on how to mitigate or avoid these issues.

2 Background on GSD Project Management

Execution of GSD projects is not new to the industry, and during the past two decades has become increasingly prevalent. Although a long list of positive effects of GSD motivates the growth of this phenomenon, GSD poses challenges both on management and technical levels [1]. The nature of software development, co-located or distributed, is widely acknowledged as a fundamentally human activity. Issues in trust, communication, and coordination over distance affect distributed team performance [2]; culture, language and time-zone obstacles [3] present in globally distributed teams can amplify these issues, impeding the effective sharing and management of team knowledge, and creating risks to project success. Successful mitigation of these risks requires extra insight, skill, and attention by the project manager.

3 Approach

We studied six cases of GSD projects within ABB, and one additional reference GSD project in a large non-ABB commercial organization. None of the cases we studied had multi-company integration situations; all of our study projects were executed within the same company. The projects were selected for diversity with regard to types of software developed, geographic distribution patterns, team sizes, number of sites involved, and development methodology (conventional or agile). Since the aim of the study was to find support for the project manager by exploring the challenges that GSD projects present for the project manager, we chose to collect the data on their experiences and perceptions through interviews and a questionnaire. In this section, the data collection and analysis methods used are presented, together with background information about the projects and respondents.

3.1 Data Collection and Analysis

The study was carried out in four steps: 1) definition of GSD metrics, 2) questionnaires, 3) interviews, and 4) analysis of data. First, available literature was examined to gain understanding of known GSD concerns, and a set of GSD metrics [4] was developed through the GQM methodology [5] to identify key measures relevant to GSD projects and project managers. To support gathering of these metrics and to complement those quantitative measures with qualitative aspects, a structured survey questionnaire (SSQ) was developed. The question set was designed to cover general context of the project (roles and responsibilities), communication and collaboration, issues perceived, and experiences gained during specific software activities. Contacts were sought with projects known to have GSD experience with a high degree of collaboration distributed over multiple countries and time zones. Six ABB projects and one external reference project were selected after initial contact interviews, covering different roles and people working from different sites in the projects. Four of the projects were studied with interviews from a broad perspective collecting the project managers' experiences as well as the project teams' views on the same situations. The majority of our interviews were done in these studies. Three projects were studied with interviews focusing more closely on the project management layer, carefully examining overall GSD issues impacting coordination between different projects and GSD strategies.

In total, 31 interviews were done with members of GSD teams located at seven sites (China, Finland, Germany, India, Norway, Sweden, and US). Each semi-structured interview lasted for about one and a half hours. Face to face interviews were done when possible; otherwise, a video or telephone conference was used (20 face to face interviews, 11 over telephone/video).

3.2 Projects Studied

The respondents reported their direct observations from one of the seven projects under study; no cross-referencing was possible since the projects were run in different parts of ABB or the non-ABB organization. In the remainder of this section, we provide a description of each project, necessarily brief because of confidentiality issues. The project names have been replaced by numbers.

Project one was a very time-critical project, divided between two sites (4.5 hours in time-zone difference). Project management, architecture tasks, and the main project team were situated at the same site; the second site was viewed as a resource center supplying less-expensive development and test services. The project manager had long experience with GSD projects (over 10 years).

Project two was divided between two sites, 7 hours in time-zone difference. Development was mainly done at one site, and delivered to the other site with a longer tradition in this type of software development.

Project three was divided among four sites, two in the same time zone; maximum time-zone difference was 11.5 hours. The development was distributed due to competencies available and where the product was produced. This project used a partially agile software development methodology.

Project four was a small team who had worked together in sequential projects for several years. The project was divided between two sites with 7 hours in time-zone difference. The project used an agile project management method. The development was distributed to better support local requirements from the markets. The project manager had long experience in project management, but only two years of experience in managing GSD projects.

Project five was divided among three sites, two in the same time zone and the third 4.5 hours away. The largest project team and the project manager were located at one site, and the smallest team was located farthest away from the other two. The project used a partially agile software development methodology.

Project six was a small project, equally divided between two sites (4.5 hours in time-zone difference); the main goal was requirement collection as preparation for a follow-on project. The reason for the division of work was not known to the project members. The project manager had relative short experience (2.5 years) with GSD.

Project seven, our reference project from a commercial non-ABB organization, was divided between two sites in the same time zone, and was planning to involve a third site (moving from no time-zone difference to a 4.5 hour difference). The division of work was based on resource and market requirements.

To complement the collected interview data and create possibilities to follow changes in the projects over time, an on-line distributed meeting questionnaire (DMQ) was designed. Data was collected from 40 participants in globally distributed meetings within ABB, partly but not exclusively by team members from the projects mentioned above. Data analysis on the information gathered from the interviews followed standard qualitative data analysis procedures [6]. Interview data were coded based partly on the categories derived from the GSD metrics (e.g. time-zone, team trust, communication, and innovation) and partly on other information which emerged (problems, needs, and positive effects).

After the first analyses, the key role of the project manager was more deeply explored. A second set of interviews and analyses focused in more detail around the project manager's tasks and responsibilities (resource handling, risk mitigation, strategies, task assignment, and collaboration). The project role coverage in these two sets of interviews is summarized in Table 1 and Table 2.

Table 1. Role coverage in interviews with GSD project team focus

Project	Roles covered
1	Project manager (1), Local team leader (2), Project team member (6), Higher management (2)
4	Project manager (1), Local team leader (1), Project team member (3)
5	Project manager (1), Local team leader (1), Project team member (2)
6	Project manager (1), Local team leader (1), Project team member (4)

Table 2. Role coverage in interviews with GSD project management focus

Project	Roles covered
2	Project manager (1)
3	Project manager (1), Higher management (1)
7	Project manager (1), Higher management (1)

In total, 4 interviews were done with higher management, 7 with project managers, 5 with local team leaders, and 15 with project team members.

4 Analysis and Discussion of Findings

All data collection was conducted between 26th of June and 11th of November 2009. The data from the DMQ will not be reported here in detail. However, one example regarding the overhead time used to schedule and set up a distributed meeting illustrates the extra effort needed. The mean overhead time was 8 minutes for telephone conference meetings, and 9 minutes for video conference meetings, spanning from zero to 16-30 min. The total overhead time reported in the 40 responses was 5.5 hours.

The most common challenges reported which influenced project manager responsibilities are summarized in Table 3. 'Culture' covers not only the predominant culture at the site location, but also the native languages and cultures of the individuals on the teams (which was not always the same as the site culture and language).

Table 3. Common GSD challenges, consequences, and mitigation strategies

Reported challenges	Example of consequences	Risk handling/Mitigation
Trust		
Competence and/or experience of people of one site questioned	People from other sites double check everything that is developed	Communicate all team members' competence and experience; if possible, job rotate team members on a regular basis to ease knowledge transfer
Communication		
Misunderstandings in the project group	Double work or low quality	Always write minutes of meetings with technical details and decisions, to ease and support communication
Create a common view	Project members do not work towards the same goal	If possible, meet and discuss goals and learn to know each other during project start up; arrange dedicated project rooms at all sites with communication equipment always up and running
Put a face to a voice	Telephone conferences harder with more misunderstandings	Meet and/or use videoconference regularly
Too little communication	Take too long to discover misunderstandings	Plan short meetings every day for task coordination and to get to know each other
Coordination		
Dependencies between sites	One problem can easily mean more problems - higher risk	Have clear borders; specify as much as possible, and keep track of dependencies
Requirements not detailed enough	Misunderstandings or double work	Set up tight collaboration with stakeholders, and see that all have enough background knowledge; if not, take actions
All sites do not follow same processes	Creates extra work	Agree on same work process from the beginning of the project
Culture		
Understanding management hierarchies/styles	Hard to know who to talk to and involve	Learn about the culture, talk to people from or familiar with the culture Use the different sites' "personality", for example: risk awareness vs. speed
Language		
Hard to understand what other says	Less communication during meetings	Try to use videoconference; support meetings with written slides; write minutes of meeting with all decisions.
Temporal barriers		
Few or no overlapping office hours	Hard to arrange meetings	Let all project members dedicate certain hours for project communications and meetings

Table 4. GSD Metric Example – Trust

GSD Metric	Aggregate Value
Trust among team members within site #1	4.4 (strong to very strong)
Trust among team members within site #2	3.0 (ok)
Site #1 members' trust of team members at site #2	1.5 (very weak to weak)
Site #2 members' trust of team members at site #1	2.7 (weak to ok)

The important planning and budget work put extra demands on the project manager for a GSD project. Examples reported include: extra time to work on specifications and descriptions; extra time to coordinate management issues between local team leaders and project manager; increased effort to administer meetings, due to time zone restrictions; extra meeting time to compensate for absence of everyday small talk.

Our recommendations for project manager support are structured in two main phases. First, we consider a startup phase, to be executed as early as possible (preferably during initial project planning) for project classification and risk identification. The second phase addresses ongoing project monitoring and control and active risk management.

The suggested startup procedure is to select key GSD measures from the set for use as risk indicators, and collect data to establish a baseline for following the selected measures during project execution. By emphasizing these measures, the importance of these issues becomes clearer for the project manager, which helps in identifying, prioritizing, and defining contingency and mitigation strategies for managing the project work. Mitigation strategies can then be selected from the recognized GSD tactics (e.g. shifting work times to minimize impact of time zone differentials, or use of a collaboration tool) to address the specific GSD-related issues which present the greatest risks to the project.

During phase two, these identified risk indicators are monitored with periodic re-measurements, enabling adjustments and corrective actions to be taken as needed. The baseline data collection and monitoring make it possible to build a knowledge base for GSD project experiences, which will become valuable as reference for future project managers in the important start up phase.

Trust measures are a good example of a GSD metric which can be useful for both initial gathering and for periodic monitoring. For instance, on one project distributed across two sites with temporal, cultural, and language differences, we gathered the data shown in Table 4 for various trust measures, using a 1-5 Likert scale (1=very weak, 2=weak, 3=ok, 4=strong, 5=very strong).

The trust metric data in Table 4 would alert a GSD-savvy project manager to act quickly to increase the trust between sites, particularly trust by site #1 members of site #2 members. Subsequent measurements would provide insight into whether the steps taken by the project manager were effective in improving trust.

A new GSD project which is now underway at ABB is applying this risk management strategy, giving us possibility for follow up study and evaluation of the impact of this strategy on project risks and execution.

5 Conclusions and Further Work

The factors affecting GSD projects can impair almost any industrial software development project. Distances do not need to be global to matter (just 30 meters of separation has effects [7] [8]), and even team members who are nominally co-located may travel to other time zones for business, and/or may have multi-cultural backgrounds.

A recent publication from Microsoft [9] which examined the impact of distributed and collocated development on product quality indicates that GSD tactics and tools did effectively mitigate the effects of distributing a project in the industrial environment for the study. However, the diversity in project characteristics and patterns of distribution of development in commercial industry justify continued investigation into which approaches are most effective under various circumstances.

Our future work will include studying GSD projects at ABB that identify and select GSD-related risk indicators, find mitigation strategies, and measure their impact. We hope to help project managers on GSD and non-GSD teams to work more effectively, and to enable other project managers to gain from this knowledge and thereby achieve higher project team performance and better business results.

Acknowledgements

The authors wish to thank the ABB and external interviewees for their participation, without which this work would not have been possible.

References

1. Sangwan, R., Bass, M., Nullick, N., Paulish, D.L., Kazmeier, J.: Global Software Development Handbook. Auerbach Publications, Boca Raton (2007)
2. Herbsleb, J., Paulish, D.J., Bass, M.: Global software development at Siemens: Experience from nine projects. In: International Conference on Software Engineering (ICSE), St. Louis, MO, USA, May 15-21, pp. 524–533 (2005), doi:10.1109/ICSE.2005.1553598
3. Herbsleb, J., Mockus, A., Finholt, T.A., Grinter, R.E.: Distance, dependencies, and delay in a global collaboration. In: ACM Conference on Computer-Supported Cooperative Work (CSCW), Philadelphia, PA, USA, December 2-7, pp. 319–328 (2000), CSCW 2000 - 10.1145/358916.359003
4. Snipes, W., Smiley, K., Krishnan, P.M., Björndal, P.: Measuring Collaboration in Globally Distributed Software Development Teams. In: Proc. First Workshop on Human Aspects of Software Engineering (HAoSE 2009) at OOPSLA, Orlando, Florida (2009)
5. Basili, V.R., Caldiera, G., Rombach, H.D.: The Goal Question Metric Approach. In: Basili, V.R., Caldiera, G., Rombach, H.D. (eds.) Encyclopedia of Software Engineering. John Wiley & Sons, Inc., Chichester (1994)
6. Miles, M.B., Huberman, A.M.: Qualitative Data Analysis: An Expanded Sourcebook, 2nd edn. SAGE Publications, Thousand Oaks (1994)
7. Herbsleb, J., Moitra, D.: Global software development, guest editor's introduction. IEEE Software 18, 16–20 (2001), doi:10.1109/52.914732
8. Teasley, S.D., Covi, L.A., Krishnan, M.S., Olson, J.S.: Rapid software development through team collocation. IEEE Transactions on Software Engineering 28(7), 671–683 (2002), doi:10.1109/TSE.2002.1019481
9. Bird, C., Nagappan, N., Devanbu, P., Gall, H., Murphy, B.: Does distributed development affect software quality? An empirical case study of Windows Vista. In: IEEE 31st International Conference on Software Engineering (ICSE), Vancouver, BC, Canada, May 16-24, pp. 518–528 (2009), doi:10.1109/ICSE.2009.5070550

The Catalan Government Prequalification Strategy for Software Development Suppliers

Josep M. Marco-Simó, Joan A. Pastor, and Rafael Macau

Universitat Oberta de Catalunya, Rambla del Poblenou, 156,
08018 Barcelona, Spain
{jmarco,jpastorc,rmacau}@uoc.edu

Abstract. This paper presents an industry practice case in public administration from Catalonia, Spain. The Catalan regional government decided in 2004 to design and enforce a prequalification strategy for their IT services vendors, in order to improve the quality of the involved outsourcing processes and outcomes. Within this wider context, in this paper we focus in the description and analysis of the specific strategy and criteria designed for pre-qualifying vendors for software development services. We explain the faced challenges and the rationale behind the criteria. These were updated in mid-2008, after the insights drawn from the first four years of experience. In fact, the Catalan Government pretends to refine regularly their prequalification strategy, in general for all IT services but more specifically for software development services. These account for the biggest part of their budget, the most varied set of service subcategories, and the greatest number of involved companies.

Keywords: outsourcing software development services, prequalification of software service suppliers, public procurement of IT services.

1 Introduction

Outsourcing of information systems, services and technologies (ISST) at public administrations (PA) has not produced a great deal of scientific literature [1,2]. We believe that this situation is paradoxical given the economical importance of the topic (in most countries PA is the biggest ISST consumer) as well as its social interest (the effectiveness in the management of public money).

In this paper we explain an in-depth case study that we are undertaking, dealing with ISST outsourcing decisions in a PA: the implementation of a strategy for the prequalification of the suppliers of ISST for the *Generalitat de Catalunya*, Catalonia's autonomous government, within Spain. This strategy was decided in 2004 and updated in mid-2008 [3], after the insights drawn from its first four years.

We will focus mostly on the prequalification for the wide range of suppliers that provide software development services to the *Generalitat*. These suppliers range from those who develop software projects almost from scratch to those who integrate existing software solutions.

M. Nordio et al. (Eds.): SEAFOOD 2010, LNBIP 54, pp. 71–78, 2010.

The paper is organized as follows. In Section 2 we detail the prequalification strategy and mechanism. In section 3 we address the case of software development services prequalification, and in section 4 we present some reflections on its initial results.

2 The Prequalification Mechanism

The prequalification mechanism under our consideration (AMH'08: *Acord Marc d'Homologació, 2008* or Homologation Framework Agreement, 2008) established four main categories (called batches) of ISST to be purchased that we summarize in Table 1. Each batch is divided in different sub-batches. A supplier could be chosen for one or more sub-batches.

For each batch and sub-batch the following points have been established: a) a foreseen monetary budget to be spent; b) a maximum number of suppliers that can be prequalified; and c) some requirements that the selected suppliers have to fulfil. These requirements include, among others, issues related to professional skills and quality certifications; methodological issues; and security issues (in the next section we will detail all these requirements in the context of the A2.1 sub-batch). For each subcategory a call for provider candidates has been made. Each candidature has then been evaluated attending these requirements (in a 100 points scale) and those suppliers who obtain a greater score are selected.

Table 1. Batches of AMH'08 [(1) Budget for the first year in millions of Euros]

Batch	Budget (1)	Sub-batches	Maximum number of prequalified suppliers
A: Software Development Services	132	12	135
B: Consulting Services	13	5	75
C: IT Deployment Services	16	3	30
D: Attendance and management of IT installations	64	5	20

At this point, the *Generalitat* has just a pool of pre-selected providers, that is to say, a list from which the final tenders for future projects will be selected from. So, every time that a department or unit of the *Generalitat* has a new project proposal belonging to a sub-batch to be launched, then the pre-selected providers of this sub-batch must present an offer for this project. This offer includes specific budget, project and technical aspects. The best offer is then selected to provide the required service through a formal process that follows the general public procurement laws.

At the end, what is expected from the AMH mechanism is that a) a significant reduction in the time needed for the adjudication of subsequent projects, and that b) the best available providers will be detected previously to actual service *CFPs (Call For Proposals).*

For understanding the final implementation of the mechanism, also in the Software Development Services Batch detailed in next section, it is necessary to keep in mind that it must answer at least three main dimensions, with often conflicting forces:

- Quality and efficiency goals, in other words, the usual interests of project managers;
- Law requirements and public administration constraints that make compulsory a lot of conditions for the transparency of the process;
- Industrial politics of the *Generalitat* government, interested in promoting the ISST sector in Catalonia.

3 The Software Development Services Batch

As we show in Table 1, Batch A is the most important in terms of economic budget volume, number of providers and number of sub-batches. How are the providers of Batch A evaluated? Each provider can achieve the maximum score of 100 points according to the following criteria:

- Up to 60 points from professional and technical resources. Among them:
  - Up to 40 from technical knowledge;
  - Up to 10 from university studies;
  - Up to 5 from industry alliances;
  - Up to 5 from quality certifications (IEC 9126, CMM, SPICE);
- Up to 25 points from the use of contrasted or certified methodologies;
- Up to 10 points from security issues (CISA, CISM, CISSP, ISO27001);
- Up to 5 points from Research, Development and Innovation practices and investments.

Batch A is divided in 12 sub-batches, summarized in Table 2. The maximum number of suppliers that can be prequalified for each sub-batch ranges from 10 to 15.

3.1 A Detailed View as Example: Sub-batch A2.1

As an example of how general evaluation criteria are applied in a sub-batch, we detail in this subsection the A2.1 sub-batch (Table 3). This sub-batch corresponds to the higher total budget foreseen (27 milions of Euros) and embraces the majority of projects involved with new software development. In fact, this sub-batch corresponds to the most demanded software technologies.

The points given to specific technical skills depend on: a) how extended is this technology within the projects of *Generalitat* and b) how interesting is this technology expected to be in the future, that is, how *Generalitat* wants to promote it. For example this is the case of J2EE, that corresponds to the technology most widely extended, as well as the case of open-source, also important in the current moment but that is promoted in order to reach a highest relevance on the medium term. Suppliers such as Oracle, Microsoft and Adobe are considered at the same level, and residual value is given to old technologies (COBOL, Power builder) still running in some not yet upgraded environments.

Table 2. Batch A. [(1) In Euros; (2) Foreseen for the first year, in millions of Euros]

Sub-batch id. and project budget thresholds (1)	Services description	Total budget (2)	Technical knowledge considered
A1.1 > 150.000 A1.2 < 150.000	Software development in host environments	2 3	DB2 IDMS COBOL
A2.1 > 150.000 A2.2 < 150.000	Software development in distributed environments	27 8	J2EE Open source .Net Oracle Adobe BEA PowerBuilder COBOL
A3.1	Software development based on integrated solutions (< 1.000.000) and Geographical Information Systems (GIS), Business Intelligence (BI) and Enterprise Content Management (ECM) solutions (>200.000)	6	ARCINFO (ESRI) Geomedia (Intergraph) Miramon (CREAF) Map Guide (Autodesk) Microstation Geographics(Bentley Systems) Smallworld (GE Energy) Microstrategy SAP-BI Dynasight MS-BI SAS-BI Other BI solutions Filenet Documentum SAP-CRM Siebel
A3.2 < 200.000	Software development based on GIS packaged solutions	2	ARCINFO (ESRI) Geomedia (Intergraph) Miramon (CREAF) Map Guide (Autodesk) Microstation Geographics(Bentley Systems) Smallworld (GE Energy)
A3.3 < 200.000	Software development based on BI packaged solutions	2	Microstrategy SAP-BI Dynasight MS-BI SAS-BI Other BI solutions
A3.4 < 200.000	Software development based on ECM packaged solutions	2	Filenet Documentum Other ECM solutions

Table 2. *(continued)*

A4.1 >200.000 A4.2 <200.000	Software development based on Enterprise Resource Planning (ERP) packaged solutions	6 1	SAP R/3 MS-Dynamics/Navision Other ERP solutions
A5.1 >200.000 A5.2 <200.000	Web portals and software development based on Content Management Systems (CMS) solutions	6 1	Vignette Tridion MS-CMS

Some discussions arose around the value given to university studies, as compared to other skills items. From the AMH it looks like having technical and short effort consuming certifications is almost as important as having full-blown scientific or engineering university diplomas. Similar discussions have been detected for top-level industrial alliances, for example those belonging to Oracle Partner Network, in relationship with quality certifications such as CMM.

On the other hand, it is clear the importance given to the use of a well justified and detailed methodology, as a way to increase the feasibility and performance of the resulting developments. In the same sense, it is also clear the importance given to security issues, also in the context of software development projects: in PA environments data security is a strategic issue given that corresponds to one of its core compulsory characteristics.

Finally, the Research, Development and Innovation issue reflects the interest of the *Generalitat* in innovative supplies that invest in their future capabilities.

3.2 Rationale Behind the Design of Batch A

There are several reasons that explain why Batch A is defined this way. Most of them must be understood from the perspective of a public administration, which often has its roots in a political trend or decision. Below we comment on the most relevant reasons behind this definition.

Amount limits. As it is shown in Table 2, in almost each sub-batch the same service is divided in two, according to a budget threshold. These limits only exist in Batch A. The main reason behind this division is the interest of the *Generalitat* for giving opportunities to providers other than the big companies. Usually it is normal that the biggest projects are assigned to big companies, often the big international corporations, and sometimes to alliances between more than one of these companies. But those companies could also be interested in small projects, especially in a crisis situation as the one that started in 2007. When that happens, SMEs (Small and Medium Enterprises) could not be able to fight with big companies and could lose the possibility to become a *Generalitat* provider. Given that the Catalan industry of software development is mainly composed by SMEs, it sounds natural that *Generalitat*, one of the main users of software development services in Catalonia, reserves a relevant part of its budget for the Catalan SME companies. That is to say, amount limits emerge from a political trend interested in giving business to local SMEs.

Subcontracting constraints. There are some subcontracting conditions that are not shown in Table 2: only the companies included in the sub-batches on the upper amount threshold are allowed to subcontract an assigned project. And, additionally: a) the subcontract only can reach 30% of the total amount; and b) the company to be subcontracted must belong to the equivalent sub-batch in the lower amount segment. For example, a company included in sub-batch A2.2 can only subcontract to a company included in the A2.1 sub-batch. These constraints are intended to: a) reinforce

Table 3. Detailed evaluation criteria for the A2.1 sub-batch

Professional and technical resources			60 points
Technical knowledge: The maximum score will be given to the provider with the highest number of professionals of each technical field, up to 300. The other providers will be evaluated proportionally to that number of professionals.		40 points	
J2EE	9 points		
Open source	9		
.NET	6		
Oracle development tools	6		
Adobe development tools	6		
BEA development tools	2		
Power builder certified	1		
Cobol development	1		
University studies (technical graduates and postgraduates): The same criteria than in *Technical knowledge*		10 points	
Industry alliances: 1 point for each top level industry alliance related to the technologies stated in *Technical knowledge*, up to 5 as a maximum.		5 points	
Quality certifications: 5 punts directly for the providers which had developed a project according to the following norms: ISO/IEC 9126; SEI/CMM (level 2 or higher) or SPICE .		5 points	
Methodology: Up to 25 points for using a specific methodology related to analysis, development, deployment and upgrading software projects for browser-based and client/server environments.			25 points
Security:			10 points
ISO27001: 3 points directly for the providers that hold this certification (or the ones that were previous to ISO27001)		3 points	
CISA, CISM, CISSP: The same criteria as in *Technical knowledge*.		7	
Research, Development and Innovation			5 points
Projects developed within well-known Research Centres: 1 point for each research project of that category developed during the last three years, up to 3 points as a maximum.		3	
Ratio of research investment over incomes: 2 points directly if it is greater than 4.5%; 1 point directly if it is greater than 3%.		2	

the amount limits logic of a sub-batch (a *political* reason); and b) limit the long chains of subcontracting that have appeared in the past (a *technical* reason).

Certified skills. One of the ways used to guarantee what is referred to as *technical competence* is by *giving points* or requiring to the prequalified providers that their human resources have certified training (in general technical skills but also in product-dependent ones), in addition to university studies. In the same sense, certifications on the whole or part of the provider organization processes are welcomed. Including those certifications in the AMH, from its first version, has had at least two consequences: a) that a demand of training on the required certifications has grown; and b) that the *Generalitat* has additional knowledge about what strengths and weaknesses have their possible providers. Most of the technical certifications, usual in the big companies, are less common in the SMEs. That reflects a software industry not used to these types of demands. In order to fill that gap, the *Generalitat* has promoted the training and certification of these skills, by funding with public money some of this training (PMP, ITIL, ISO 20000, CISM, ISO 27002) and by achieving lower prices from the training companies. In some way the *Generalitat* pushes the demand for this training, but also presses the trainers to offer an accessible training service to the industry, from economic and organizational points of view.

Required methodologies. The main methodologies required or valued in the AMH'08 are related to project management and to software development processes. These requirements linked to the tradition of some public administrations (we recall here for example *Euromethod* [4], promoted by the EU; or *Merise* [5] developed by the French PA). In addition to that, the *Generalitat* promotes *ESPRIT*, an internal methodology conceived for project management but that is also clearly grounded on software development practices. As a consequence of that, it is a feasible argument that the importance given by public sector to the software development process can be explained by the historical big investments on not successful software projects.

4 Some Reflections on Initial Results

At the time of writing this paper it is not possible to analyze the results obtained by AMH'08 because it is just fifteen months old and not too many projects have been finished using this mechanism. But among the available objective data, in Table 4 we summarize the resulting data about the origin of the company capital of the selected providers. What is interesting of this data is that the AMH'08 consolidates a model where local industry has a very relevant paper. That is to say, that the near sourcing strategy (for Catalan and Spanish companies) has been consolidated and that this strategy gives chance to the big suppliers, but also to SMEs. Of course, most of the multinational companies that have also been prequalified have their own presence in Catalonia or in Spain and also most of them have adapted to the local market.

Another result of the AMH strategy is its impact on the supplier prestige. In fact, some of them state that, after being prequalified by the *Generalitat*, their business volume has increased among other customers, specially other PAs that have adhered to the *Generalitat* AMH'04 results. In fact, other public administrations –local ones, mainly- consider *Generalitat*'s prequalified providers as tested and reliable providers for their needs. But, on the other hand and for the same reason, not having reached the prequalification has implied for some companies the loss of some business chances.

Table 4. Origin (expressed in %) of prequalified providers by A sub-batches

Origin	A1.1	A1.2	A2.1	A2.2.	A3.1	A3.2	A3.3	A3.4	A4.1	A4.2	A5.1	A5.2
Catalonia	10,0	20,0	13,3	33,3	0,0	30,0	44,4	44,4	0,0	25,0	0,0	33,3
Rest of Spain	70,0	10,0	46,7	20,0	55,6	0,0	33,3	33,3	70,0	25,0	60,0	22,2
Other	20,0	70,0	40,0	46,7	44,4	70,0	22,2	22,2	30,0	50,0	40,0	44,4

5 Conclusions and Future Work

In this paper we have contextualized a real case in PA where the main strategy for dealing with procurement of ISST services is that of prequalification prior to actual selection of providers. We have focused on software development services, explaining in detail their prequalification criteria, rationale and origins.

We have seen that the mechanism tries to translate to objective indicators the technical and political objectives of *Generalitat*: quality of the selected providers, promotion of technical issues and support to local industry. The result is a mechanism that can be evolved according to emerging needs and detected problems (in fact, its third version is being developed at the moment of writing this paper).

In the future, as data is captured on the perceived or estimated quality of service from users and from stakeholders in general, additional more detailed analyses will be possible to show the effects of the prequalification strategy and mechanism, as it has been applied in the studied case.

Acknowledgments. Our sincere thanks to Jordi Amat, Jordi Bosch, Josep Checa, Xavier Manuel, Sergi Marcén, Daniel Marco, Tomàs Roy and Josué Sallent, all of them executives at *Generalitat* that have facilitated us access to and insight into data, as well as access to the rest of stakeholders of the case.

References

1. Marco-Simó, J.M., Pastor, J.A., Macau, R.: Public procurement of IS/IT services: past research and future challenges. In: Proc. of the 11th IFIP TC8 WG 8.6 International Working Conference (2008)
2. Vilvovsky, S.: Differences between public and private IT outsourcing: common themes in the literature. In: Proc. of international conference on Digital government research (2008)
3. AMH 2008 (2008), `http://www.gencat.cat/economia/ambits/contractacio/ccs/` (last retrieved: 10/01/2010)
4. Helmerich, A.: Euromethod Contract Management. In: Bernus, P., Mertins, K., Schmidt, G. (eds.) Handbook on Architectures of Information Systems. Springer, Heidelberg (1998)
5. Tardieu, H., Rochfeld, A., Colletti, R.: La méthode Merise - Tome 1 Principes et outils. Editions d'organisation, Paris (1983)

On Knowledge Services for Outsourcing Professional Development

Dehua Ju[1] and Beijun Shen[2]

[1] Application Solutions & Technologies, Inc. (ASTI), Shanghai 200233, China
asti-gm@online.sh.cn
[2] Shanghai Jiaotong University, Shanghai 200240, China
bjshen@sjtu.edu.cn

Abstract. In this paper the authors analyze and discuss the opportunities and challenges in the development of outsourcing professionals. Through systematic investigation, with reference to emerging new learning models and insights, the authors proposed a novel solution to migrate from traditional training to knowledge services via an ICT-based public platform. The paper described the basic infrastructure of the Public Knowledge Service Platform and its main functions. To assure quality knowledge services the content design is utmost importance and a BOKs-based framework is proposed to support learner-centric design and learning on demand. A case study is shown to illustrate how to implement a rational public knowledge services platform for outsourcing Professional development, including a provider-oriented Outsourcing Professional Body Of Knowledge (OPBOK) developed in the proposed project.

Keywords: Knowledge Service, Outsourcing Professional Development, Life-long Learning, Professionalism, Body of Knowledge (BOK), OPBOK, On-the-Job Learning, Learning On-Demand.

1 Introduction

Outsourcing is the mainstream in current world economy and also a hot topic in China's software community. Based on Atkearney's Global Service Location Index (GSLI) 2005, 2007 and 2009, India, China and Malaysia remained top three attractive destinations for global service outsourcing. Facing with the global multisourcing trend, China has great opportunities to enter outsourcing market. In 2006 Chinese government put forward the ambitious "1000-100-10" project [1] to develop the service outsourcing industry. The state strategic policy has actuated a high growth rate in outsourcing business and also brought on a clear gap in the human resource supply-demand chain accordingly. In 2009 the State Council released a new file on promoting the development of the service outsourcing industry and named 21 national service outsourcing cities, aiming at a multi-tier development, all of which have built their Outsourcing Training centers or Institutes. For how to foster qualified outsourcing professionals, there are many issues that remain to be solved.

First, what is the qualification of outsourcing professionals? The growth in outsourcing profession has led IAOP (International Association of Outsourcing Professionals) to

M. Nordio et al. (Eds.): SEAFOOD 2010, LNBIP 54, pp. 79–86, 2010.

release the Outsourcing Professional Body of Knowledge (OPBOK) [2] and Certified Outsourcing Professionals (COP) program in 2006. However, we found this OPBOK was more client-oriented. For Chinese side we need a provider-oriented model.

When talking the talent issue, a conventional thinking always expects much from universities, but the university graduate is just an entry workforce, not solving whole HR problems in outsourcing business at all. Chinese have a proverb: "Distant water can't quench a nearby fire". To improve the competence, we should also consider how to enhance skills of on-the-job employees, which is a continuous education issue, a very weak area in China compared with India. The main bottleneck constrained our development is mainly the lack in senior and middle-level professionals. Some foreign clients made a pointed remark to us: "We just concern about how many qualified project managers you can train, rather than programmers".

The booming economy has stimulated a learning wave among most Chinese people for improved work and life. Class teaching is the most prevailing learning model in China. However, high cost and resource constraints (qualified teachers, available time, facilities etc.) of the traditional training class restrain its development. There is a high demand to invent an open learning environment for free access with much lower cost.

For all these challenges and problems, we need a proactive strategic solution, not only rely on reactive methods. How we can do that? We need some 'Out-of-Box' thinking based on some recently emerging insights and trends.

2 Some Key Viewpoints

Before describing the HR solution framework suggested by us, it had better declare some key viewpoints underlying that in order to reach a common understanding on the design principle. The following basic principles are simply adhered:

- It should be a lifelong learning (LLL) system, instead of an additional university, which can also provide learning support for working staff towards high-end interdisciplinary professionals.
- Promote professionalism, internationalization and standardization in outsourcing professionals development for which the domain body of knowledge (BOKs) is recommended as a reference professional skills standard.
- Adopt new learning models and platforms which is learner-centric rather than teacher-centric to support on-demand knowledge acquisition and ICT-enabled for more open access.

3 From Training to Knowledge Services

To promote technology transfer, we released a technology resource website called 'IT Source' (www.ITURLs.com) in 2002 which quickly became an attractive IT website in China. Many young admired it 'a real help'. After first surprise, we recognized such a fact that even we published only what we have collected, our work help them saving the time for doing similar thing. We called it as 'Knowledge Service Reuse', that is, one's labour exempts others from repeated works. This inspired us to do 'Knowledge

Services' idea. For technology transfer, it is just enough to touch a little bit of terms and points. For knowledge transfer, we need a much comprehensive collection, maybe based on the domain body of knowledge, that will be a much greater value for learners.

In knowledge economy, knowledge is the first resource and knowledge is power! Knowledge services will be the main infrastructure and key component of knowledge economy to enhance the human capital. There are many discussions and studies on the term 'Knowledge Service' in the world literature [3], such as in the Library 2.0 and building Web of Knowledge. Although there are some similarities, our considerations will focus on how to organize a dedicated effort to build an open accessible and shared learning platform for helping professional development. We noticed that Knowledge as a Service (KaaS) [4] has being emerged as a new interesting topic, in which an on-demand, bite-sized, where-needed approach to knowledge acquisition is stressed on.

4 Public Knowledge Service Platform

Why we proposed a solution so-called "Public Knowledge Service Platform" ?

Because it can give full play of IT Advantages, through Internet, implement dissemination and nationwide sharing of knowledge resources and promote formulation of Communities of Practice. It can realize the e-Knowledge [5] and Intelligent KM, turning originally scattered and isolated information into organic knowledge, then transforming it again into an open and accessible information resource. By fully utilizing centralized resources and sharing the common service functions of the platform, it can readily implement one-stop service and integrate cross-domains knowledge for fostering interdisciplinary talents.

For design of the knowledge service platform, we identified five main functions so far, or called as five centers, they are: (1) Technology Transfer Center; (2) e-Learning Center; (3) Knowledge Resources Center; (4) Consulting Center; and (5) Communities Center.

In the following sections, we will discuss the last three centers in more details.

4.1 Knowledge Resources Center

As an authoritative knowledge source, its development must have robust backup expertise to cover enough wide spectrum and degree of depth in its knowledge resources. To ensure high quality and keep updated contents, a dedicated professional team for knowledge services is a must, including qualified domain experts' participation. One solution suggested for that purpose is to fully apply available Body of Knowledge of related domains (BOKs) as a scientific guide in collecting knowledge resources.

The key for KaaS is having knowledge at the time of maximum opportunity [4]. Thus, the priority in the platform development is put on what demanded most from society development – a learner-centric design. Based on our own background, the current focus is put on the following main domains:

- the SE domain urgently required by developing software industry;
- the IT domain urgently required by implementing state informatization strategy;

- the New Product Development & Innovation domain urgently required by building the Innovation-Oriented country

To gain a solid foundation for developing knowledge service platforms, we started our R&D project from systematically searching, collecting, studying, compiling and developing related BOKs. In the three main domains mentioned above, so far, we have gathered 132 associated BOKs in total.

This center is very similar to the web of knowledge, a centralized knowledge resources repository based on these BOKs. Guided by the interested BOK, the learner can easily access what knowledge points/areas he/she wants to know. The resources repository provides an one-stop services just simply via a browser. Its user likes entering a specialized reading room with very rich collections and can learn anything what he/she wants. We refer this function as "A Learning Paradise for IT Talents". A resource collection efforts have been launched in parallel with the 'first things first' principle. A dozen of special domains have begun to take sharp already, such as:

- SE domain: Software Architecture, Requirements Engineering, Project Management, Quality Management, Software Testing, SWEBOK;
- IT domain: ITSM/ITIL, Information Security;
- Innovation domain: New Product Development, Innovation Methods, Knowledge Management.

Besides these resources, we have also developed abundant training materials in our e-Learning center for three domains mentioned above, including 228 e-learning modules with 60270 .ppt pages – a valuable knowledge asset for a variety of learners as an entry shortcut. All these resources will help users to fulfill a 'self-paced' learning with on-demand knowledge acquisition.

4.2 Consulting Center – On-the Job Learning (OJL)

In this center we are planning to provide so-called 'On-The-Job Learning' or 'Contextual Learning', a more interesting and valuable learning platform – a new direction of next-generation learning environment. Learn while working/learn by doing, learn for better job will be very attractive to all enterprises as it can provide performance support either. Learning for Use and Use after Learning will bring about a high-motivation learning and help much deeper grasp. It looks like that a teacher, expert, master or knowledge base always accompanying you, providing online and real-time assistance.

The Figure 1 shows a development process of the new learning platform in which you can find the related BOK will also act an important role that ensure the knowledge collected can fully cover all key points in the domain workflow and the keywords presented in all knowledge points will help for an ontology -based search.

4.3 Communities Center

This On-the-Job Learning platform has all advantages of contextual learning systems. More important is that it can promote the construction of Community of Practice (CoP). It is really an open system and community. After wide trail by thousands users, the drawbacks and problems of applied systems can be fully exposed and new solutions

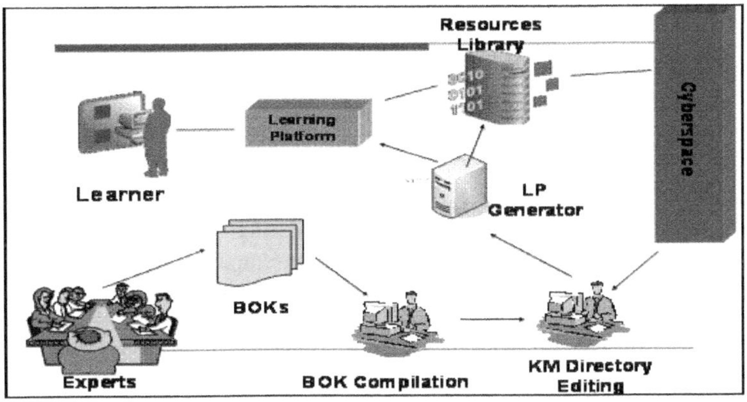

Fig. 1. The On-the-Job Learning Platform

and improvements can continued. Even in the case of no satisfied answer from the system, the requester still can call for a 'SOS' help via internet from other CoP members, including e-mentors/e-coaches as well as peer practitioners. In fact, the platform has accomplished three virtual links within same CoP: A link to leading experts in CoP through the domain BOK development; a link to worldwide experienced CoP members during collecting knowledge resources written by them; and a physical link to active CoP members for peer cooperation while involving in an idea and experience exchange.

This platform will be a participatory web supported by web 2.0 technology, facilitating knowledge and experiences sharing and promoting collaborative learning and working. Each member is not only a learner, but also a contributor which will recommend new knowledge contents and experiences as well as the feedback for system improvement. The emerging new technologies and applications will dynamically expand the related BOKs. All these will enhance and perfect the collective knowledge repository at the end.

A significant feature of this kind of platforms is that the knowledge service pushes networking to its extreme points, embodied in three aspects: It can connect different platforms together to form a ubiquitous, accessible in any time and interoperable shared application environment, including wireless access through 3G. It can link originally scattered and unorganized information into complete and organic knowledge assets and then turn them into easily accessible information and send knowledge services into everybody's hands. It can tie members of CoPs together to formulate a collaborative learning & working environment – co-building a learning community for society's progress.

5 The Service Platform for Outsourcing Professionals

As an active response to the demand on outsourcing professional development (OPD) in China, we promptly released our knowledge services platform project for OPD based on our R&D achievements under the target flag 'From Process Maturity to People Maturity'.

To do so, we have engaged in following efforts and made significant progress:

5.1 Body of Knowledge Development

The first task is to identify what knowledge and skills the outsourcing professionals should require, i.e. related Body of Knowledge.

After doing a comprehensive survey on training models for outsourcing professionals, we found quite scattered solutions. Even each one has its merits and specific views, lack of unified framework is obvious problem. In view of these problems, we tried to integrate these existing models for assimilating the best of them. Now we have compiled a draft of OPBOK, which is provider-oriented and can be used as a starting point of our outsourcing knowledge service platform project.

For developing our own OPBOK, we studied and referred the following main BOKs and models: IAOP OPBOK[2], CMU/ITSqc eSCM [6], IIOM OMBOK [7], and NASSCOM NAC [8] etc. The design guideline behind the OPBOK is as follows: Outsourcing is technology/knowledge intensive job; outsourcing is service; outsourcing is business; outsourcing is management practice; outsourcing focuses on people factor; outsourcing is a global activity with new challenges. Based on these recognitions, we follow the framework of CMU's eSCM model to re-organize the OPBOK into five management, which avoid overlaps appeared in many existing models. They are: Business Management, People Management, Technology/ Knowledge Management, Global Project Management, and Service/Operation Management.

Outsourcing is an emerging multidiscipline which needs T-sharp professionals, i.e. having both broad and deep knowledge: speaking the language of many disciplines, and being deep in at least one area. A good outsourcing professional knows not only software development, also has management experiences, can do a better service and even deep domain knowledge able to deliver innovative solutions to clients. To make this happen, the outsourcing knowledge resources repository should gain backup from a wide variety of related bodies of knowledge. To reflect latest technology development and market demands, we expand timely our BOK-base, for example, adding new knowledge points like agile project management (APM) and global project management (GPM) as well as necessary soft skills into original PMBOK to adapt new needs in outsourcing development. Recently we also started cooperation with JUSE (Union of Japanese Scientists & Engineering) to jointly promote their Software Quality Body of Knowledge (SQuBOK) just released.

5.2 Outsourcing Knowledge Resources Repository

As a rational solution, we designed a quite rich Outsourcing Knowledge Resource Repository (Fig.2). As seen in the figure, all the main components are BOK- or standard-based to ensure the integrity of knowledge contents. In addition to CMMI-based SPI knowledge popular in current China, we also increased new contents to meet other enterprise certification needs, such as for ISO 20000, ISO 27001, ISO 15504 (SPICE), and eSCM etc. The underway development of resources collection includes JUSE's SQuBOK and ISTQB's Certified Tester Foundation Level and Advanced Level. The total volume of will exceed over 30,000 URLs.

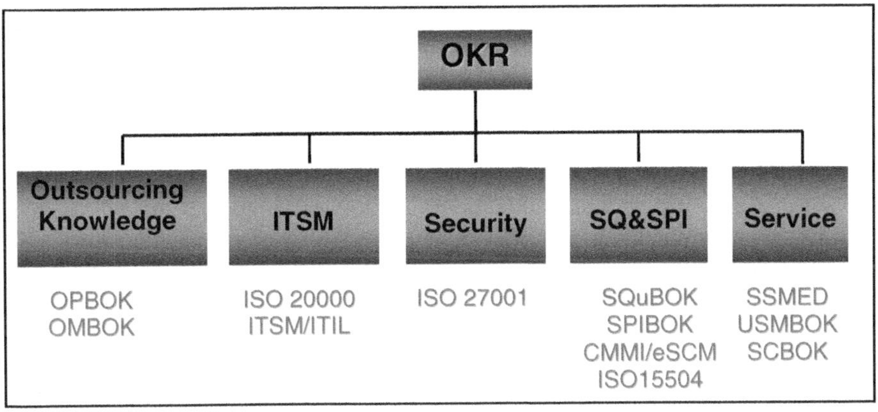

Fig. 2. Outsourcing Knowledge Repository

Besides the knowledge resources, we also provided 38 optional course modules with 7523 .ppt pages of training materials in the e-Learning center which pay high attention on management practices required in outsourcing business to meet varied needs of different outsourcing professional roles, as shown in Table 1.

Table 1. Optional Course Modules Provided

Area	Course Modules
Business-Management	New Trends, India Model, Business Model, Partnerships, Global Delivery Model, BTO, KPO
Marketing	Branding, Due Diligence, Pricing & Negotiation, SLA/SLM, e-Marketing
People Management	P-CMM, Knowledge Worker, Code of Ethics, Mentoring
Capability Maturity	CMMI, eSCM, SPICE, 6 Sigma, COPC-2000, SEPG, PSP/TSP
Management-Practice	GPM, Service Management, OMF, QA, SW Testing, SPC, Security , ITSM/ITIL
Knowledge-Management	KM in Outsourcing, Cultural Competence, OPD, UML

6 Conclusions

Knowledge service is a key component and essential infrastructure of knowledge economy era. Knowledge is a crucial resource in promoting modern industries and economy.

In this paper, we analyzed the problems and challenges in current HRD and outsourcing professional development, and then proposed a novel solution for professional development, suitable for SE, IT, Outsourcing and other possible domains. The key part is to design the Public Knowledge Service Platform. In addition to the system architecture, the stress is put on the content design to ensure quality knowledge services for which a BOKs-based framework was proposed. Not just contents, the second consideration is to build a support platform for learning and applying knowledge in the context. Networking or social engineering is another focus to help building knowledge enabled CoPs. The platform design proposed fully embodies the '5C' nature combination of e-Knowledge [3], i.e. Content, Context, Community, Connection and Computer-supported Collaboration, which greatly enhance the value of knowledge services. It provides an ideal, open, low cost, ubiquitous, easily accessible lifelong learning support environment for HRD urgently needed, to enable personalized learning on-demand.

Outsourcing professionals are a group of T-sharp multidiscipline knowledge workers. The public knowledge service platform proposed with comprehensive resources will like a stretch of fertile land with rich knowledge nourishment to speed up their growth and mature.

References

1. Chinese Ministry of Commerce: Circular of Ministry of Commerce on Implementing the Thousand-Hundred-Ten Project (2006), `http://chinasourcing.mofcom.gov.cn/content2.jsp?id=19654`
2. IAOP: Outsourcing Professional Body of Knowledge, OPBOK (2006), `http://www.outsourcingprofessional.org/firmbuilder/articles/34/175/1196/`
3. Norris, D.M., Lefrere, P., Mason, J.: Making Knowledge Services Work in Higher Education. EDUCAUSE Review 41(5), 84–101 (2006)
4. cumulusIQ: Knowledge as a Service (KaaS) Enables the Right Action, Right Now, `http://marketing.cumulusiq.com/Knowledge_as_a_Service`
5. CORDIS: i-KnowS Integrated e-Knowledge Services, `ftp://ftp.cordis.europa.eu/pub/ist/docs/ka3/eat/i-knows.pdf`
6. CMU/ITSqc: The eSourcing Capability Model for Service Providers (eSCM-SP) v2, `http://itsqc.cmu.edu/models/escm-sp/index.asp`
7. IIOM: Outsourcing Management Body of Knowledge, OMBOK (2009), `http://www.cio-index.net/Channels/IT_Sourcing/IT_Sourcing_Articles/IT_Sourcing_View_Article/ArticleId/1707/Outsourcing-Management-Body-of-Knowledge-OMBOK-1707.aspx`
8. NASSCOM: NAC - NASSCOM Assessment of Competence, `http://nac.nasscom.in/`

A Structured Framework for Managing Offshore Outsourcing Risks on Software Support Projects

Natacha Lascano[2], Sebastián Maniasi[1], and Pedro Colla[1]

[1] HP Enterprise Services, BestShore Applications Services Argentina, Av. La Voz del Interior 7050, Córdoba, Córdoba, Argentina
{pedro.colla,sebastian.maniasi}@hp.com
[2] Motorola Argentina Software Center
Hipólito Yrigoyen 146, Córdoba, Córdoba, Argentina
natacha.lascano@motorola.com

Abstract. Offshoring software is being increasingly used by the IT industry since companies pursue the value derived from this model. At the same time, the distributed operation is more complex as it creates specific processes, technology, support, communication, quality risks and issues to address. As this list grows, part of the value obtained might then be destroyed together with the returns originally forecasted. The actions derived to manage the involved risks must be perceived as essential components to be inspected during the execution of any offshoring project. This paper addresses this topic by proposing a structured framework to identify and understand these risks and to facilitate their mitigation. Focus is placed on software support since a particular set of considerations needs to be examined. The proposal is then consolidated in a group of practices to perform a structured risk management. Application examples, conclusions and further work needed are discussed.

Keywords: Offshoring, Software Support, Outsourcing Risks, Ongoing Production Support.

1 Introduction

Offshore project development has gained prominence in recent years as a viable means of IT outsourcing [1]. It is mainly employed to reduce development costs and improve staffing options. The economic case is an important aspect to be considered and the results, as they will be discussed in this paper, are subject to substantial considerations. What can not be disputed is that the IT industry is changing and rapidly driving companies to adopt such practices [2] [3] [4] [5].

Organizations trying to tap on the benefits of offshoring face many risks and challenges. As a number of studies show, about 40% of offshore software development projects end being flop [6]. Almost 80% of the projects face problems at different stages of the lifecycle [3]. Even small and medium sized enterprises are increasingly engaging into offshoring activities where some key competitive advantages of this segment –such as the flexible use of coordination methods, high adaptation, and customer retention– need to be preserved in a context of spatial and temporal distribution of the work [7].

M. Nordio et al. (Eds.): SEAFOOD 2010, LNBIP 54, pp. 87–95, 2010.

Efforts from several authors help to understand the factors beneath the risks, and ultimately the issues, experienced by enterprises from a wide perspective. Even when studies show companies achieved goals of enhanced market, increased capabilities and access to talent by doing offshore projects; there were found several structural risks such as loss of knowledge, IP protection issues, ability of providers to cope with rates of turnover, lack of requirements flexibility, and absence of business know-how by the offshore team [3] [8].

Inadequate management of risk is a major reason for exceeding a project's estimated time and cost. On top of the natural risk any given technology project has, any attempt to perform development activities by a team of people from many countries, speaking a variety of languages and separated by time and distance have higher risk. Advances in communication and technologies enable cooperative work but research in such fields as psychology, organizational behavior, management and communication have found that such work in the global environment has limitations. It seems that managing the project, vendors, and contract in the international context increases the risk. Companies face an elusive inverse relation between risk and cost where attempts to mitigate one increases the other [9].

Although much of the bibliography concentrates into determining the best way for enterprises to understand and mitigate the risks associated with sending work overseas, it is also true that companies receiving offshore work need to understand and mitigate their own set of risks in dealing with remote partners while ensuring their reputation is preserved [10] [11].

2 Background

Software development is the set of activities through which user needs are translated into a computer application [12] while the ongoing production support is the process of operating and maintaining that computer application over time in order to ensure the successful operation of the system [13]. Specifically, ongoing support will be referred in this paper as the work intended to respond to events in production environment that will require outsource resources to attend them on unplanned basis.

Most of the bibliography concentrates on the risk profiles derived from transferring development work to offshore providers ([3] [9] [11]) but little is being said about using this strategy for ongoing production support activities [14]. However, the bulk of the IT budget resides on the support of their existing applications and consequently it concentrates most of the saving opportunities originated from the cost competitiveness of offshore promises. A closer inspection shows this kind of activity also pushes the factors to be considered for the initiatives in the direction of higher risks.

In order to tackle all the aspects mentioned before, this paper proposes a systematic approach to understand, evaluate and mitigate risks on the receiving organizations during the ongoing support.

Typically, production support differs from development projects since the first involves: short delivery cycles, direct access to production environments, personalized service, more straightforward configuration and release management schemas, and guaranteed response time to all inquiries.

Particularly, offshore development teams normally lack product ownership so they receive a somewhat well defined set of requirements or specifications to implement. Their technical competences will play then the main role in construction phase. On the other hand, production support services will require not only technical abilities, but also functional operations and business knowledge. This is it, in order to understand the feasibility and business criticality to fix a production problem. As a consequence, the functional understanding of the software will be the key for success as it will determine how offshore groups effectively deal with support requests.

In this context, successful development projects relay on its *Definition and Initialization* phase (involving requirements definition and scheduling) since work can be carefully depicted and broken-down to early determine user needs [15]. In contrast, production support activities, as an ongoing process, may not be easily foreseen up front and this forces offshore groups to get acquainted with regular operations in order to cope with critical or complex unplanned events. As a result, this service will highly depend on how the offshore teams assimilate that functional knowledge making the proper execution of the *Transition* or *Knowledge Transfer* phase crucial [15].

2.1 Risk Management and Investment Returns

Moving offshore activities related to production support requires longer investment horizons for a viable return to be obtained making them long term propositions. Any financial analysis of such investment will involve the evaluation of the value projected to the present in order to ensure it is a viable proposition.

Different investment strategies with the same outcome on the same subject would trend from a pure numerical perspective to yield the same value once normalized by their risks [16]; under that approach, the differential cost productivities achieved by going offshore would then be mapped into a risk high enough to arbitrate the value to be equal among the different alternatives. Reality is much more complex than the views allowed by a pure financial perspective and the organization does obtain additional value by adopting offshore practices because of the possibility to tap on additional resources, access flexible staffing methods and even, in some cases, leverage the time zone differences [6].

However, the existence of risks produces uncertainty in the achievement of the planned outcomes, and this variability requires for the investment to demand higher returns to be justified [1] [17]. This mechanism can be seen as equivalent to destroy some of the value created by the offshore proposition. It is then very important to mitigate the identified risks in order to protect the value of the offshore investment.

Little [18] also brings the notion of "*saving detractors*" which are specific to the offshore activities depending on project nature, labor and cultural frameworks and the strategy that drives the move. Once it has been assessed the magnitude of the risks involved, this author also brings the concept taken forward in this paper: the characterization of those risks is the key to define the mitigation strategies to apply.

3 Key Proposal

This paper concentrates on the perspective of a particular location part of a global services provider that can offer diverse solutions from different places.

In that scenario, offshore propositions suffer from excessive focus on short term issues without a long term view towards a common goal; this paper also considers the total value of the project as such goal and the risk mitigation as the strategy to preserve it.

Finally, this paper also proposes the idea to segregate the methodologies used for offshoring development and production support work as they deal with fundamentally different business and technical risks that require specific mitigation actions.

3.1 Risk Identification – Risk Dimensions

Risk management is a very important part of the software engineering field and there exists a large body of work in this area [19] [20]. Using taxonomies and grouping risks on categories helps to identify, analyze, and monitor them [21]. Even when these categories are typically associated with traditional project management areas (such us schedule, costs, and quality), the framework proposed is based on clustering those categories into two main dimensions determined by the necessity of acquiring or transferring specific knowledge. Also, as an additional benefit, the clustering provides to the executives making the decisions, the ability to compare vastly disparate alternatives in a comprehensive way to grasp the essence of the risks associated.

Technical Risks. Include those associated to the uncertainty of meeting one or more requirements related to some technical aspect of a software system. In order to assess their significance it is necessary to identify the technological and procedural requirements of the computer application and to compare them with the available experience. Examples of the categories comprised on this dimension are: technology, hardware requirements, licensing, connectivity, and process maturity matters.

Business Risks. Include those associated to the uncertainty of meeting one or more requirements related to some business aspect supported by a software system. In order to determine their importance it is necessary to understand the particularities of that activity, the strategic impact of the computer application, and the level of existence of previous comparable experience on the provider company. Examples of the categories comprised on this dimension are: legal, finance, staff, security, cultural and business continuity matters.

3.2 Risk Assessment – Severities Definition

The severity of the risks is generally determined by two factors: (1) the impact of the possible adverse consequences and (2) their probability of occurrence.

The first action is to analyze these factors for each one of the risks identified on the technical and business dimensions in order to weigh them. Among all the many different tools available, risk matrices provide a structured and intuitive way to complete this process [22].

As a second step, it is necessary to combine the risks' severities inside each dimension in order to generically evaluate the two of them and, in the end, to select a proper mitigation strategy.

3.3 Risk Planning – Mitigation Strategies

The offshore moving of production support expand the dimensions to be considered into technical and business ones; any given proposition could then be assessed on the relative risk on each dimension and mapped into such space. In this paper, we will propose common strategies to mitigate risk based on that mapping.

The proposed risk quadrants are depicted in the Figure 1.

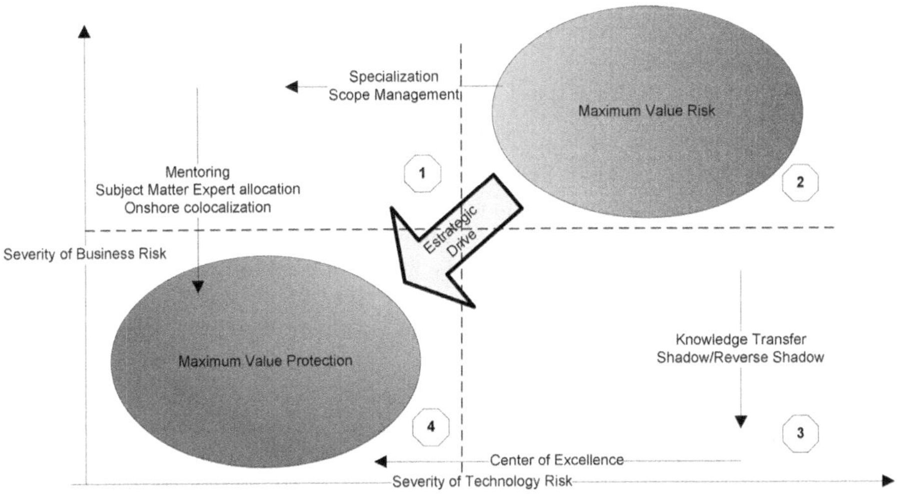

Fig. 1. Risk Space for Offshoring Production Support

The organization would naturally have an interest in minimizing all the risks associated with their offshoring projects, which means trying to move it into the area where both the business and technical risks are minimum ("*Maximum Value Protection*" area).

At the same time this is especially true if the proposition is assessed as being in the high risk area ("*Maximum Value Risk*") where the destruction of value will be maximized. Business or technical constraints might prevent a full mitigation strategy to be implemented.

The risk assessment can hardly be described as dominated by a single factor, it is much more like the weighting of several ones, and therefore the risk mitigation might convey the implementation of several initiatives. Each initiative in turn can mitigate a specific risk being included in the business or technical dimensions of the analysis. Fortunately, the experience helps to identify certain generic actions to be useful to mitigate specific risks; these actions can be grouped as follows:

Business Risks Mitigations

Actions that reduce the risks grouped in the business dimension are among others:

- To produce a structured transition management following a well defined and proven process as opposed to an ad-hoc grouping of tailored activities.

- To plan for extensive knowledge transfer lead by key experts on the onshore team and secure their availability in advance.
- To collocate few resources at the onshore location to enhance communications; complex interactions can be handled on early stages of the project when remote interactions just cannot cope with the needs of stakeholders.
- To include shadow and reverse shadow activities during the transition.
- To apply segmented support processes with clear interfaces and entry/exit criteria.
- To comply with business needs by means of a globally distributed team.

Technical Risks Mitigations
Actions that reduce the risks grouped in the technical dimension are among others:

- To introduce specific training programs at technical and process levels.
- To deploy a certification or Center of Excellence (CoE) strategy.
- To define and implement an onshore central repository of information in order to preserve the collective experience and the knowledge acquired which are vital to deliver on production support scenarios and are subject to specific threats such as personnel rotation or rapid growth.
- To establish a well defined software support process and track compliance thru metrics and indicators.
- To create mentoring programs driven by onshore subject matter experts, in some case even lasting well after all formal transition activities were completed.
- To found a virtual and global technical community through the new communication facilities and mechanisms.

Some of these actions will be more suitable depending on the particular assessment in the risk space a given project might have. In any case, since actions normally take time to be applied, the order of the actions does influence the final outcome; as such, all actions should receive an early categorization between being "*quick wins*" or "*low hanging fruits*" and actions that will be deployed over larger periods that might require investment decisions.

4 Application Examples

4.1 Case 1: Outsourcing in a Personal Computer Security Software Company

Context: Company A (a global major personal computer security software corporation) decided to outsource and offshore with Company B (a leader business and technology services corporation) its applications production support to further align its IT area with new business tendencies.

Risk Identification & Assessment: Several risks were identified in both, technical and business dimensions; the following are very relevant in the context of this paper:

- *Lack of immediate available assistance during the critical monthly billing cycle.*
  - Business Dimension – high probability and high impact: major business areas were distributed on different countries, and the original proposal implied to

transfer the production support services to a single offshore location not aligned in time zone with all of them.

- *Lack of knowledge in offshore of base applications technologies.*
  - Technical Dimension – medium/high probability and high impact: vital systems were coded with uncommon and leading edge technologies.

After combining all the risks' identified on each dimension, Company B positioned this project up-right in the 2nd quadrant of the proposed model ("*Maximum Value Risk*" area).

Risk Planning: The major actions selected by Company B to move this project into the "*Maximum Value Protection*" area can be summarized as follows:

- *Lack of immediate available assistance during the critical monthly billing cycle.*
  - To distribute the responsibility to deliver the production support service across three different sites located on shifted time zones.
  - To implement a variety of contact mechanisms for providing to the customer a permanent and redundant access to the production support group.
  - To institutionalize a common handover process to promote the continuity of the production support service.
- *Lack of knowledge in offshore of base applications technologies.*
  - To introduce in the offshore locations specific and focused certification training programs on the most relevant and exceptional technologies.
  - To establish a common knowledge repository for both courses and technical lessons learnt.
  - To deploy a global escalation process to provide enduring access to senior technical resources.

Results: The transition period was kept in the planned three months timeframe with an associated cost fairly close to the estimated one without major issues. Support has been distributed in the offshore sites for the last 2 years.

4.2 Case 2: Mentoring in a Business and Technology Services Company

Context: Company A (a leader business and technology services corporation) decided to internally transfer the production support responsibility of an external customer's development environment to a new offshore location in order increase its capacity while keeping the associated costs under control.

Risk Identification & Assessment: As the customer's development environment was built with standard languages and techniques, no significant risks on the technical dimension were identified; even though, the following risk on the business dimension is very relevant in the context of this paper:

- *Lack of compliance with the processes to access/correct the environment.*

- Business Dimension – high probability and high impact: a highly complex, extensive and strict process was required by the customer in order to perform any task over its operative development environment.

After combining all the risks' identified on each dimension, Company A positioned this project up-center in the 1st quadrant of the proposed model.

Risk Planning: The major actions selected by Company A to move this project into the "*Maximum Value Protection*" area can be summarized as follows:

- *Lack of compliance with the processes for accessing/correcting the environment.*
  - To assign experienced onshore resources for more than 6 months in the offshore location in order to validate the compliance with the process and to effectively spread their knowledge through this area.
  - To tailor and use a proven and formal knowledge management framework in order to guarantee the detailed review of the main aspects of the process.
  - To establish a shadow and reverse shadow periods intended to avoid major disruptions on the supported development environment during the initial phases of the new support schema.

Results: The offshore team has been consistently managing the support of the development environment for the last three years while the sustain efforts were increased as per customer's request with no impact on the financials (provider nor customer).

5 Summary

Efforts to move offshore software development work face challenges which lead to outstanding risks for the project; these risks need to be mitigated in order to protect the value of the investment. Ongoing production support augment some of the risks factors such as cycle time, requirements definition and communication but it still is the bulk of the workload in need of being transferred. This paper moves the discussion one step further by outlining a simple model to evaluate the risks in the business and technical dimensions. Once the prospect project is characterized in these terms, several generic mitigation activities are proposed to move into delivery parameters which are less risky and, ultimately, to move the entire proposition to a delivery model that minimizes the overall risk. Several cases are provided.

Future work could concentrate on further defining the model to provide a structured way to compute the relative magnitude of the risks involved, and propose a set of performance indicators to measure the results of the risk mitigation efforts on the transition process.

References

1. Balaji, S., Ahuja, M.K., Ranganathan, C.: Offshore projects: Assessing the Effect of Knowledge Transfer Requirements and ISD capability. In: Proceedings of the 39th Hawaii International Conference on System Sciences, pp. 1–10 (2006)
2. Kobayashi-Hillary, M.: A passage to India. QUeue, 56–60 (2005)

3. Iacovou, C., Nakatsu, R.: A risk profile of offshore-outsourced development projects. Communications of the ACM 51(6), 89–94 (2008)
4. Aspray, W., Mayadas, F., Vardi, M.Y.: Globalization and Offshoring of Software - A Report of the ACM Job Migration Task Force. ACM, New York (2006)
5. Jaakkola, H.: Towards a Globalized Software Industry. Acta Polytechnica Hungarica 6(5), 69–84 (2009)
6. Betz, S., Stephan, R.: Offshoring of Software Development - Methods and Tools for Risk Management. In: International Conference on Global Software Engineering, ICGSE (2007)
7. Boden, A., Nett, B., Wulf, V.: Articulation work in Small-Scale Offshore Software Development Projects. In: Cooperative and Human Aspects of Software Engineering, pp. 21–24 (2008)
8. Huen, W.H.: An enterprise perspective of software offshoring. In: 36th ASEE/IEEE Frontiers in Education Conference, S2C-17-22 (2008)
9. Sakthivel, S.: Managing Risk in Offshore Systems Development. Communications of the ACM 50(4), 69–75 (2007)
10. Taylor, H.: The move to outsourced IT projects. Key Risks from the provider perspective. In: SIGMIS-CPR, Atlanta, pp. 149–154 (2005)
11. Islam, S., Joarder, M., Houmb, S.: Goal and Risk Factors in Offshore Outsourced Software Development from Vendor's Viewpoint. In: Proceedings of the 2009 Fourth IEEE International Conference on Global Software Engineering, pp. 347–352 (2009)
12. IEEE Standard Glossary of Software Engineering Terminology/IEEE Std 610.12-1990. Institute of Electrical and Electronics Engineers, New York (1991)
13. Harvey, S., Weaver, B.: Applying CMMI to a Production Support (Software Maintenance) Environment. Software Engineering Institute, Pittsburgh (2004)
14. Webster, K.P.B., de Oliveira, K.M., Anquetil, N.: A Risk Taxonomy Proposal for Software Maintenance. In: Proceedings of the 21st IEEE International Conference on Software Maintenance (2005)
15. Betz, S., Mäkiö, J., Oberweis, A.: OUTSHORE Maturity Model: Assistance of Software Offshore Outsourcing Decisions. In: Proceedings of APMS Innovations in Networks. IFIP (2008)
16. Brealey, R.A., Myers, S.C.: Principles of Corporate Finance, 7th edn. McGraw Hill Higher Education, New York (2002) ISBN 0071151451
17. Harrison, W., Raffo, D., Settle, J., Eickelmann, N.: Making a business case for software process improvement. Software Quality Journal 8(2) (1999)
18. Little, T.: Assessing the cost of Outsourcing: Efficiency, Effectiveness and Risk. 1-4244-2537-2/08 2008 IEEE, pp. 95–100 (2008)
19. Jones, C.: Assessment and Control of Software Risks. Prentice Hall, Englewood Cliffs (1994) ISBN 0137414064
20. Ray, W.: New directions in Risk Management. SEI (2003)
21. Carr, M., Konda, S., Monarch, I., Ulrich, F., Clay, W.: Taxonomy-Based Risk Identification. SEI (1993)
22. Lansdowne, Z.F.: Risk matrix: an approach for prioritizing risks and tracking risk mitigation progress. In: 30th Project Management Institute Seminars & Symposium, Philadelphia (1999)

Author Index

GPSR Compliance

The European Union's (EU) General Product Safety Regulation (GPSR) is a set of rules that requires consumer products to be safe and our obligations to ensure this.

If you have any concerns about our products, you can contact us on ProductSafety@springernature.com

In case Publisher is established outside the EU, the EU authorized representative is:

Springer Nature Customer Service Center GmbH
Europaplatz 3
69115 Heidelberg, Germany

Batch number: 10854054

Printed by Printforce, the Netherlands